Ch —

support of the Foundation. I hope Practical EBM helps you "Get to the Truth!"

Larry Baker brings a world of experience and a wealth of knowledge to the critical subject of enterprise risk management. In his inimitable storytelling fashion, Larry does exactly what he promises to do: Get to the truth. Larry's book should be on the required reading list of all in the profession who seek to add value to their organizations by managing risks in an increasingly complex environment.

—**Richard F. Chambers, CIA, QIAL, CGAP, CCSA, CRMA**
President and Chief Executive Officer
The Institute of Internal Auditors
Lake Mary, FL

Larry Baker is one of the pioneers of ERM as he has been involved in helping organizations strengthen their risk oversight long before many of us had ever heard the term "enterprise risk management." The insights from his years of helping organizations integrate their risk efforts into the context of their organization's strategy provide valuable perspectives of tactical approaches that can help to ensure ERM is value-adding. This books helps business leaders see how ERM, if done right, should be an important strategic tool for both management and boards as they strive to enhance the value of the organization for its stakeholders.

—**Mark Beasley**
Deloitte Professor of ERM and Director of the ERM Initiative
Poole College of Management
North Carolina State University
Raleigh, NC

PRACTICAL ENTERPRISE RISK MANAGEMENT

PRACTICAL ENTERPRISE RISK MANAGEMENT

GETTING TO THE TRUTH

Larry L. Baker, CRMA, CCSA, CPA

"…when asked about the value of ERM, one CEO I worked with summed it up in a few simple words: 'It gets to the truth.'"

Copyright © 2018 by the Internal Audit Foundation. All rights reserved.

Published by the Internal Audit Foundation
1035 Greenwood Blvd., Suite 401
Lake Mary, Florida 32746, USA

No part of this publication may be reproduced, stored in a retrieval system, or transmitted in any form by any means—electronic, mechanical, photocopying, recording, or otherwise—without prior written permission of the publisher. Requests to the publisher for permission should be sent electronically to: bookstore@theiia.org with the subject line "reprint permission request."

Limit of Liability: The Internal Audit Foundation publishes this document for informational and educational purposes and is not a substitute for legal or accounting advice. The Foundation does not provide such advice and makes no warranty as to any legal or accounting results through its publication of this document. When legal or accounting issues arise, professional assistance should be sought and retained.

The IIA's International Professional Practices Framework (IPPF) comprises the full range of existing and developing practice guidance for the profession. The IPPF provides guidance to internal auditors globally and paves the way to world-class internal auditing.

The IIA and the Foundation work in partnership with researchers from around the globe who conduct valuable studies on critical issues affecting today's business world. Much of the content presented in their final reports is a result of Foundation-funded research and prepared as a service to the Foundation and the internal audit profession. Expressed opinions, interpretations, or points of view represent a consensus of the researchers and do not necessarily reflect or represent the official position or policies of The IIA or the Foundation.

ISBN-13: 978-1-63454-013-1
22 21 20 19 18   1 2 3 4 5

CONTENTS

Foreword xi

Acknowledgments xv

About the Author xvii

Introduction 1

Chapter 1   Setting the Stage 7

Chapter 2   Management-Value Approach: Strategic Risk Assessment 19

Chapter 3   Management-Value Approach: Strategic Risk Analysis and Action Planning 37

Chapter 4   Board-Confidence Approach: Enterprise Risk Inventory 55

Chapter 5   Board-Confidence Approach: Enterprise Risk Analysis 65

Chapter 6   Board-Confidence Approach: Enterprise Risk Assessment 79

Chapter 7   Board-Confidence Approach: Enterprise Risk Workshops 93

Chapter 8   Key Risk and Performance Indicators 109

Conclusion 117

Glossary 119

Internal Audit Foundation Sponsor Recognition 121

Internal Audit Foundation Board of Trustees 123

Internal Audit Foundation Committee of Research and Education Advisors 125

LIST OF EXHIBITS

Exhibit 1.1: ERM Objectives 12

Exhibit 2.1: ERM Framework - Management-Value Approach 20

Exhibit 2.2: Risk Management Process 23

Exhibit 2.3: Timeline for Risk Management Process Step 1: Risk Assessment 24

Exhibit 2.4: Example Enterprise Risk Inventory for the Management-Driven Approach. 26

Exhibit 2.5: Pre-Read Worksheet 29

Exhibit 2.6: Summary of Key Risks 32

Exhibit 3.1: Timeline for Risk Management Process Step 2: Risk Analysis and Step 3: Reporting and Action Planning 39

Exhibit 3.2: Risk Analysis/Action Planning Summary Template 42

Exhibit 3.3: Strategic Risk Analysis/Action Planning Detail Template. 44

Exhibit 3.4: ERM Framework - Management-Value Approach 50

Exhibit 4.1: ERM Framework - Board-Confidence Approach. 56

Exhibit 4.2: Example Risk Inventory with Sample Enterprise Risks 62

Exhibit 5.1: Completed Example Enterprise Risk Inventory. 68

Exhibit 5.2: Inherent Risk Summary Form. 70

Exhibit 5.3: Environmental, Health, and Safety Example Inherent Risk Summary: Health and Safety. 73

Exhibit 5.4: Example Executive Summary: Environmental, Health, and Safety 76

Exhibit 6.1:	Survey Screen Introducing the Survey Criteria	84
Exhibit 6.2:	Example Screen of Survey Questions	85
Exhibit 6.3:	Enterprise Risks Prioritized	87
Exhibit 6.4:	Comparing Priorities by Respondent Group	88
Exhibit 6.5:	Enterprise Risk Heat Map	89
Exhibit 7.1:	Grouping of Enterprise Risk for the Inventory	95
Exhibit 7.2:	Example Inherent Risk Handout for the Workshop	98
Exhibit 7.3:	Rating Scale for Workshop Questions	99
Exhibit 7.4:	Opportunity Gaps	101
Exhibit 7.5:	Post-Workshop Survey	105
Exhibit 7.6:	Example Survey Results	106
Exhibit 8.1:	Example Executive Dashboard	113
Exhibit 8.2:	KPI Framework	114

All exhibits and templates are available in a format that you can customize to meet the needs of your organization. To access online, please use the following link:

www.theiia.org/practicalERM

FOREWORD

By Charlie Wright

The first time I met Larry Baker was in Tulsa, Oklahoma, in 2009. He had invited me to an enterprise risk management (ERM) roundtable that he had organized for business leaders in the region. I was immediately impressed not only by his extensive experience consulting with some very large companies but his ability to articulate a sensible approach to ERM. I came to learn that he was a true pioneer in the field of ERM. I noticed that Larry had a genuine and engaging presentation style that allowed him to communicate complicated ideas in a simple, matter-of-fact way. But, even more than all of that, the trait I observed that most stood out about him was his ability to "get to the truth."

Since that initial meeting, I have had the pleasure of getting to know Larry quite well and we have collaborated in many different ways. I have been through his training on risk management and internal audit topics. He helped me establish high-functioning, well-respected ERM at a $10 billion energy company. We have been co-workers as well as fellow committee and taskforce members. Larry recently joined The IIA as a member of the Executive Leadership Team. So now, in my volunteer role on the Executive Committee of the Global Board of The IIA, we are working together again to advocate for the profession and help meet the needs of internal auditors around the globe. He seems to inherently know how to modify his style per the scenario and its needs to add value in all of these roles. However, regardless of which hat he is wearing at any particular time, he is always an evangelist for the value of implementing strong risk management.

Larry is intensely adamant about the fact that executing ERM effectively will add value to your organization. Just like me. In fact, as the firm-wide leader of the ERM practice for BKD CPAs & Advisors, one of the nation's largest professional services firms, I am now doing much of the same type of consulting that Larry has been doing for years. One of the things I have learned is that executing ERM effectively is not an easy task and the "right" way to implement ERM is different for every organization. Fortunately, Larry's substantial experience working with executives at many different companies allows him to identify various components of ERM that enable risk managers to create an effective risk management framework regardless of the facts and circumstances.

I have worked for three very interesting *Fortune* 500 companies throughout my career and all of them have operated in an extremely complex risk environment. A major pipeline company with a brilliant strategy redeployed its previously decommissioned pipelines to be used as conduits for fiber optic cable. The execution of the new subsidiary seemed to be managed relatively well, but too much supply and too little demand eventually led to its bankruptcy, leaving investors with financial losses and many employees with shattered dreams.

One of the largest, most well-managed airlines in the world was responsible for safely flying thousands of passengers around the world at 35,000 feet in a "rocket" filled with jet fuel. However, the economics of competing in an industry where practically all the major players had gone bankrupt was too much to overcome and the airline eventually filed for bankruptcy itself and was acquired by a smaller competitor.

An exploration and production company invested billions of dollars toward exploring for oil or gas hidden deep beneath the surface of the earth in hard-to-reach pockets of rock. The product is highly flammable and under such tremendous pressure that it occasionally explodes and shoots thousands of pounds of steel pipe out of the ground like toothpicks. Then, when fuel prices collapsed, they had to lay off a significant number of employees to continue operating.

What is the common thread that caused all these previously very successful companies to run into financial distress resulting in layoffs and bankruptcies? They all failed to mitigate their business risks in one way or another. They could not get to the truth fast enough. Larry has written this book to help risk managers understand the key components of establishing a successful ERM framework and setting up an effective approach to avoid a similar fate while adding significant strategic value.

Foreword

I'm sure it's obvious by now that Larry has the knowledge and experience to address this topic. He is a consummate professional: experienced, knowledgeable, articulate, and, lucky for us, willing to share his learnings with the rest of us. He has a vast repertoire of relevant, useful stories—many of which he has sprinkled throughout this book. One of the characteristics I enjoy most about Larry is his ability to use storytelling to convey difficult and complex concepts.

I am fortunate to call Larry an associate, colleague, and close friend. I commend Larry for taking time to pull together such a practical collection of real-world experiences, tools, techniques, and approaches to facilitate the development and execution of successful ERM. I highly recommend *Practical Enterprise Risk Management: Getting to the Truth* and predict this book will be required reading for risk managers, chief audit executives, board members, and other executives who desire to make sure their organizations really do "Get to the Truth."

—**Charlie T. Wright, CIA, CPA, CISA**
Director, Enterprise Risk Solutions
BKD, CPAs and Advisors

ACKNOWLEDGMENTS

Wow, what an experience, writing this book after 20 years of being in the enterprise risk management (ERM) trenches with courageous colleagues by my side while we pioneered ERM in some of the world's greatest companies. Having over two decades of success with ERM wouldn't have been possible without such amazing support of my family, business partners, and friends.

First, I must thank my teenage sweetheart, high school football queen, and wife of over 30 years, Stacy, for her continuous love, support, and understanding as I accumulated over two million airline miles to provide ERM insight and direction to leaders across the world. Second, I don't have enough space to fully share how proud I am of our three outstanding children, Kyle, 24, Lauren, 19, and Hayden, 13. I cannot ask for a more committed, loving, and successful young man and young woman than what my two older children have grown up to be. And, yes, our youngest is also on a path of success like his big brother and sister. Thanks for loving Dad, even though he traveled much and worked such long nights and weekends at times, more recently including the writing of this book.

Well, Dad, this is a BIG circle! Thank you, Frank Baker, for being a great father who always challenged me, encouraged me, and motivated me to take the world on with passion and confidence. Your motivational sports talks not only impacted my football and baseball careers, they equally impacted my collegiate and business careers. OK, now the hard part, thanking my Mom, who went on to heaven much sooner than we were ready. I know you, Nancy Baker, are smiling down on me, yes, your son who could do no wrong, at least in your eyes! You are the perfect example of what a loving mom should be. Thank you for everything. We miss you, Mom. Also, I want to thank my wonderful parents-in-law, Harry and Linda Dail, who have supported me since I was 16 years old, watched our children when we needed a helping hand, and driven hundreds of miles across the country to watch their grandchildren play sports.

Now on to my colleagues who have worked beside me over the years. Although there are many, I want to mention the few who had a great impact on me as both a professional and a person. First, I must go back to 1992 when my chief audit executive, Jim Mitchell, sent me to Canada to learn about control self-assessment as a fourth-year internal audit professional. What an impact one week had on the rest of my career. Next, I must let some of my closest colleagues and friends know how much I appreciate their support, commitment to success, and long hours we put in together as we exceeded client expectations over and over and over again during our ERM journey—Greg Hopkins, Chris McCarthy, Jeanette York, Rodger Graham, and a host of others. And, most recently, Charlie Wright continues to be a great colleague and mentor who allowed me to bring all my ERM experience to Devon Energy as we jointly developed, evolved, and sustained one of the most effective and efficient approaches to ERM I have experienced over the years. I also greatly appreciate the following colleagues who provided their ERM insights through manuscript review of my book: Tania Stegemann and Angie Chin, along with Greg, Jeanette, and Charlie.

Writing this book would have been impossible without the support of Richard Chambers, Cyndi Plamondon, and Bonnie Ulmer. Thank you for providing me an opportunity to give back to our profession. And, I appreciate your sending me all over the world this year, which allowed me to write much of this book while up in the peaceful blue skies. As for my colleagues at the Internal Audit Foundation and The IIA, our team remained flexible with my busy schedule helping me cross the finish line through effective project management, editing, typesetting, marketing, publishing, and ultimately selling my book. Many thanks to Erika Beard, Lee Ann Campbell, Candace Sacher, Cathleen Kwas, Robert Breen, and Hong Williams. Great job team!

Last, but clearly not least, I want to send a special heartfelt thank you to my new business partner and friend, Jane Seago, right out of my home town, Tulsa, Oklahoma. What an amazing experience it was working with you as you helped me sort through over 40,000 hours of ERM experience and organize my thoughts and experience into one, practical, how-to book. Hey Jane, we did it!

ABOUT THE AUTHOR

Larry L. Baker, CRMA, CCSA, CPA, is an accomplished and high-impact internal audit and risk management executive with over 40,000 hours of hands-on, real-world enterprise risk management (ERM) experience. He has been a featured speaker and member of The IIA for 30 years, providing thought leadership through global IIA committees, international and national conference presentations, and best practice articles.

Recognized as an early U.S. pioneer of ERM and control-self assessment (CSA), he has teamed with executive management to identify, measure, and report strategic risks and operational issues for many of the world's largest organizations. Larry also has deep experience with financial and operational audits, COSO frameworks, CSA, and complex company-wide special projects with *Fortune* 500 companies.

At The IIA, Larry is a member of the executive leadership team. He leads content strategy and retail operations for the Internal Audit Foundation, which provides timely insights that address the needs of our stakeholders globally. He also teams with The IIA's global leaders to develop The IIA's global strategic plan.

Prior to joining The IIA, Larry was a senior leader/partner at two *Fortune* 500 companies, two Big 4 CPA firms, and a global consulting firm. He had the privilege and challenge of building national ERM practices for Deloitte and Ernst & Young, and helping evolve the global ERM practice for Marsh & McLennan/Oliver Wyman. Most recently, Larry led the development and evolution of ERM at Devon Energy, a *Fortune* 250 company.

INTRODUCTION

Enterprise risk management (ERM) specialists, internal auditors, risk management professionals, and many other leaders help management keep its finger on the pulse of changing and emerging risks in a dynamic world. Although emerging risks can sneak up on an organization with catastrophic impact, equally important are known risks that are changing without appropriate management attention or appreciation. ERM was created to help management meet the challenge by identifying significant risks, effectively managing those risks, and adding value to the organization through better achievement of objectives.

As an early ERM pioneer, I can still vividly remember hearing, "ERM is just another fad you consultants dreamed up to make money." Well, that was more than 20 years ago and ERM is more alive and well today than ever before. Why? Because when done right, it works.

> Throughout this book, I will share my real-world experiences and ERM approaches, tools, and techniques that have resulted in better decision-making and generated significant value for some of the world's greatest companies.

ERM "done right" means value must be recognized by key stakeholders, including executive management and the board. Some struggle with the challenge of determining how to measure the value of "keeping something bad from happening." Although I recognize that challenge, I usually take a different approach to measuring ERM value. The value of ERM should be measured on how well we help management manage risks, make better strategic decisions, enhance performance, and achieve objectives that matter most to executive management, the board, and other key stakeholders. Over the years, I have heard many executives, board members, and other stakeholders acknowledge ERM value after seeing the results.

Let me share one of my favorite ERM experiences. A chief operating officer (COO) of a *Fortune* 500 manufacturing company made a 180-degree turn regarding his view of ERM shortly after the initial step—strategic risk assessment—was completed. When first introduced to ERM, he said, while wringing his hands, "All you risk guys want to do is get us all worried about stuff so we do nothing." After seeing the results of the strategic risk assessment, he said, "This is all about my business. I will put the best of the best on ERM going forward!" Why? Because we helped him and his executive team "get to the truth" about what risks could have a significant impact on the achievement of his strategic plan that had just been released.

> In fact, when asked about the value of ERM, one CEO I worked with summed it up in a few simple words: "It gets to the truth."

Among several significant risks identified, one was summarized as "potential failure of achieving significant revenue growth due to overreliance on core customers." The core customers of the company's recreational products happened to be baby boomers. While the strategies aimed at achieving tremendous growth, the baby boomers were expected to grow too old over time to keep enjoying the recreational vehicles. The COO said, "We thought about threats while developing our plan and we discuss strategies and issues with management continually; however, it took ERM to bring this critical risk to our attention." Over time, the company developed and implemented meaningful action plans to address the risk and increase the likelihood of achieving projected revenue growth, including modifying their products to attract a more diverse set of customers. Years later, I read an article with the following headline, "Manufacturing Company survives the economic downturn due to diversification of its customers." That, to me, is real ERM value.

Why This Book?

Back in the beginning years of ERM, there was little to no guiding material for us to use. Today, there is an overabundance of ERM material suggesting one approach after another, offering one opinion after another, and providing an endless number of techniques and tools. That is why, after years in the trenches with ERM, I have chosen to write this practical book.

Why will reading this book be useful to you? Most importantly, it is because this book was written *by* an ERM practitioner *for* the ERM practitioner and all others who are trying to help their companies manage risks across the enterprise. I have worked in both consulting and the corporate environment acquiring an estimated 40,000 hours of hands-on, real-world ERM experience. I had the privilege and challenge of building national ERM practices for two of the Big 4 CPA firms, helping evolve the global ERM practice of one of the world's largest insurance brokers, providing ERM services to dozens of *Fortune* 1,000 companies across industries, and most recently leading the development and evolution of ERM at a *Fortune* 250 company. Although we all continue to grow with ERM, my experience with initiating, evolving, and sustaining ERM for two decades gives me a good idea of what works and what typically does not work.

Most organizations are aware of the need to get a firm grasp on understanding and addressing their enterprise risks, but many lack an effective, sustainable approach to ERM that has been customized to fit the company culture and management style. Realizing the complexity and velocity of risks in today's dynamic global environment, those charged with developing, evolving, and leading ERM no longer have time or interest for pure theory, comparisons of generic frameworks, or a recounting of every possible approach to ERM. They need concise, focused, practical help they can begin using almost immediately. I suspect you feel that way too, or you would not have picked up this practical book.

What's in the Book?

Within these pages you will find no philosophical discussion about the nature of risk or minutely detailed charts of statistics obtained through yet another survey. Instead, you will learn about practical, tested ERM techniques and templates that will help your organization identify significant risks and determine which risks warrant management's attention. ERM, when done right, provides management ample opportunity to take action to better manage key risks toward achieving the company's objectives. I will share situations encountered while implementing and leading ERM, lessons learned, and factors that can influence the success of an ERM implementation or evolution.

No one author or one book can possibly tell you everything you need to know about ERM or all the possible ways to implement, evolve, or sustain ERM. To help you know what to expect in the following chapters, provided below are some key points about what this book *is* and what it is *not*.

What it *is*

- A "how-to" application of approaches that have worked very well for many organizations of different sizes and industries.

- A step-by-step description of two practical approaches to ERM, including supporting forms, tools, and templates that I have used with multiple companies.

- Customized ERM using terminology preferred by management, some of which may not align with more accepted terminology used by ERM practitioners or highlighted in globally accepted frameworks.

What it is *not*

- A step-by-step implementation of ERM based upon the Committee of Sponsoring Organizations of the Treadway Commission's (COSO's) ERM Framework, International Organization for Standardization (ISO) 31000 framework, or any other specific framework.

- A compendium of theoretical tools or sophisticated techniques that "could be" or "should be" used for ERM.

- A summary of an "ideal" ERM approach that claims to be effective for all organizations.

> This book discusses proven steps of initiating and evolving sustainable ERM, including activities such as:
> - Facilitating an effective strategic risk assessment
> - Completing a deeper analysis of broadly stated strategic-level risks

- Identifying key risks to the execution of your company's strategic plan
- Using risk assessment results while developing the strategic plan
- Performing an effective and efficient enterprise risk assessment
- Completing a thorough enterprise risk analysis
- Communicating the most significant risks to executives and the board in a meaningful, actionable way
- Developing a customized and relevant enterprise risk inventory
- Identifying emerging risks through effective risk workshops
- Facilitating development of action plans
- Making practical use of key risks and performance indicators
- Building and sustaining ERM using a customized ERM framework

In short, this book provides practical, how-to instruction on successfully initiating, executing, and evolving ERM.

Who Should Read It?

I realize the range of target audiences for this book is quite broad, both in tenure and level of responsibility. It targets those professionals who are responsible for leading, executing, and evolving ERM, such as chief risk officers (CROs), vice presidents (VPs) of ERM, directors of ERM, ERM specialists, strategic planning leaders, corporate risk managers, and internal auditors. It is also intended to guide those who have an interest in helping management identify, assess, and manage risk across the enterprise and increase the likelihood of achieving company objectives. Regardless of job title and ERM experience, it is possible to learn something new about

> Through ERM, we have a great opportunity to help leaders make the best decisions possible, better manage risk, and increase the likelihood of achieving objectives.

ERM every day. I am convinced that there will be something of value for you in the upcoming chapters, whether you are on your first day of being assigned to ERM or you are well into your own ERM journey.

When, not *if*, we are successful, we will be contributing to the strategic direction and long-term value of our companies.

CHAPTER 1

SETTING THE STAGE

This chapter covers a variety of topics that are presented, for the most part, in brief, easily digested sections. Each of the topics is critical to understanding this book and successfully implementing ERM.

What Is ERM?

Although ERM has been around for a couple of decades, there continue to be multiple views regarding how it is best defined. One of the definitions I have referenced occasionally is COSO's. Its most recent definition of ERM is:

> "The culture, capabilities, and practices, integrated with strategy-setting and performance, that organizations rely on to manage risk in creating, preserving, and realizing value."[1]

While that is a good definition of ERM, and one I support, I tend to put it in layman's terms, especially while talking with management and employees:

> "ERM provides timely, useful risk information that helps management make decisions and effectively manage risks toward the achievement of objectives."

Risk has been around even longer than ERM and continues to be defined in many ways. One definition that I support, also from COSO, is:

> "The possibility that events will occur and affect the achievement of strategy and business objectives."[2]

---

1 *Enterprise Risk Management – Integrated Framework* (Jersey City, NJ: Committee of Sponsoring Organizations of the Treadway Commission, 2017).
2 Ibid.

Once again, in practice, many of us try to define risk in its simplest form to facilitate effective discussions with management and employees at all levels. Over the years, I have typically defined risk as "any potential activity or event that could have a negative impact on the achievement of objectives." This simple definition has been proven effective with executives through front-line employees year after year and company after company. I recognize that risk can have an upside, but in practice, it has been simpler for risk to be discussed with management as a negative event, while considering any upside as an opportunity to better manage a risk toward the achievement of objectives.

For the purposes of this book, enterprise risk is defined as "any significant activity or event that could have a negative impact on achieving objectives across all categories of risk, such as strategic, operational, legal, and financial." Enterprise risk tends to be more significant to executive management, board members, and other key stakeholders.

> This is a good time to share my viewpoint on how to best refer to ERM, and perhaps how not to refer to ERM. I try to limit calling ERM a program or project because both terms sound temporary, with a definite end. I even limit my references to ERM as a process or system because I see ERM ultimately as an integrated part of the business. Finally, I never refer to ERM as a pilot, which tends to infer trying something with hopes it might work. Of course, none of these terms is wrong to use. Ideally, however, I prefer to refer to ERM simply as ERM, with projects being a part of ERM, especially in the early stages of implementation. Leading ERM must be a persistent commitment to proceed and to succeed, no matter how many times you get knocked down along the way—and the terms used to define and describe it must reflect that commitment to long-term success.

Two Proven Approaches

I believe most risks and issues are known among the employees across the organization. The challenge has been, and continues to be, getting those employees to speak up and getting management to listen. My strong belief is that, for most organizations and most risks, somebody, somewhere, knows something. Hence, as risk specialists, we must develop and execute ERM in a way that gets the right information, to the right people, at the right time.

> Somebody, somewhere, knows something.

ERM, done right, gives management and employees across the organization ample opportunity to share what they know, in a safe environment, with confidence that management will seriously consider the truth and take action as needed. It is common to discuss ERM at the strategic and executive level. However, I want to emphasize that this philosophy applies at every level of the organization and with every level of employee, from the chief executive officer (CEO) through frontline employees.

Most who have been practicing ERM for many years will agree that there is no "best way" to do it. However, there certainly are some approaches that have been proven effective at well-known companies and private organizations across industries for many years. This book focuses on two such ERM approaches. Before proceeding, I want to provide a little explanation about the titles I chose to use for the approaches:

> As risk specialists, we must develop and execute ERM in a way that gets the right information, to the right people, at the right time.

- The titles are intended to provide a simple way to distinguish one approach from the other as you read about both approaches in the subsequent chapters. Despite the title, most important is for you to understand that each approach requires support from both management and the board.

- The approaches actually have more commonalities than differences. In both approaches:
  - ERM is owned by management.
  - The board provides risk oversight.
  - ERM is focused on objectives.
  - ERM is strategic in nature.
  - It is possible to achieve any of the ERM objectives listed in **exhibit 1.1**.

Now, let's summarize the two approaches.

The management-value approach (covered in chapters 2 and 3): The management-value approach tends to be championed by executive management for the primary purpose of creating business value and a secondary purpose of helping the board fulfill its risk oversight role. It generally emphasizes the need to drive value through the identification and resolution of significant residual risks (risks that remain after risk management activities are taken into account) that could hinder the achievement of objectives and goals communicated to shareholders and other stakeholders. As you consider which approach may be best suited for your company, the following ERM objectives (as described in **exhibit 1.1**) tend to be of highest priority for the management-value approach:

- **Risk-informed strategic decisions**—ERM helps the organization's executives make strategic decisions based on consolidated, timely, relevant, and reliable risk information.

- **Achievement of organization's strategic objectives**—ERM increases the probability of achieving the organization's strategic objectives.

- **Risk-based capital allocation**—ERM provides a process in which capital is allocated considering the risks associated with the investment.

The board-confidence approach (covered in chapters 4 through 7): The board-confidence approach is also championed by executive management but for the primary purpose of helping the board fulfill its risk oversight role and a secondary purpose of creating business value. It generally focuses on gaining board comfort that management understands, communicates, and manages all significant risks to the organization. As you consider which approach may be best suited for your company, the following ERM objectives (as described in **exhibit 1.1**) tend to be of highest priority for the board-confidence approach:

- **Board comfort and confidence**—ERM provides comfort to the board that it is apprised of the most significant risks potentially impacting creation and protection of shareholder value.

- **Reduced reputational damage and operational surprises**—ERM reduces the occurrence of surprises and noncompliance with laws and regulations through ongoing risk management activities.

- **Portfolio view of risks**—ERM taps into risk knowledge of the organization's management to provide a consolidated and summarized portfolio view of strategic risks.

Based on my experience, the management-value approach is more commonly used, particularly due to its emphasis on assessing risks against strategic plans and objectives. It is intended to quickly focus on residual risks, whereas the board-confidence approach initially focuses on a holistic view of all critical risks, including risk inherent to the business before considering risk management activities. Both approaches focus on strategic objectives and can work for about any company across industries.

Fully implemented ERM can achieve a number of ERM objectives. I commonly use the 10 ERM objectives shown in **exhibit 1.1** to help executive management determine the most important objectives it wants to accomplish with its customized ERM. The order in which the objectives appear in **exhibit 1.1** is the order in which I have most commonly seen them ranked by executives across companies and industries. To help you determine the best approach for your company, I recommend you prioritize these objectives in an order that is most appropriate for your executive team and company culture.

Exhibit 1.1: ERM Objectives			
Ranking	**Objective Title**	**ERM Objectives**	**Primary Stakeholders**
1st	Board Comfort and Confidence	ERM provides comfort to the board that it is apprised of the most significant risks potentially impacting creation and protection of shareholder value as well as increasing director and officer liability. Consistent process to assess, manage, monitor, and report enterprise risks provides the board with confidence that management is responding appropriately to the most significant risks.	Board/AC Chair, CEO
2nd	Risk-Informed Strategic Decisions	ERM helps the organization's executives make strategic decisions based on consolidated, timely, relevant, and reliable risk information. Executives apply risk information in a strategic setting based on a standard risk management process and consistent tools.	Board/AC Chair, CEO, Executive Management
3rd	Achievement of the Organization's Strategic Objectives	ERM increases the probability of achieving the organization's strategic objectives by prioritizing strategic risks and resolving contributing factors directly linked to the achievement of the strategic objectives.	Board/AC Chair, CEO, Executive Management

Exhibit 1.1: ERM Objectives (continued)			
Ranking	**Objective Title**	**ERM Objectives**	**Primary Stakeholders**
4th	Reduction of Reputational Damage and Operational Surprises	ERM reduces the occurrence of surprises and noncompliance with laws and regulations through ongoing risk management activities executed at the functional and business process levels of the organization. ERM facilitates timely evaluation and resolution of potentially unfortunate events, thereby minimizing damage to the organization's reputation, product quality, competitive advantage, and/or financial results.	Board/AC Chair, CEO
5th	Portfolio View of Risk	ERM taps into risk knowledge of the organization's management to provide a consolidated and summarized portfolio view of strategic risks that transcend the organization's operations and support functions.	Board/AC Chair, CEO, Executive Management
6th	Risk Management Functional Synergies and Efficiencies	Alignment of risk functions' strategies, goals, and objectives provides synergies and streamlining benefits, thereby reducing costs and minimizing duplicative or conflicting efforts across the organization (e.g., internal audit; legal; human resources [HR]; environmental, health, and safety [EHS]).	Executive Management, Functional Heads

Exhibit 1.1: ERM Objectives (continued)			
Ranking	Objective Title	ERM Objectives	Primary Stakeholders
7th	Risk-Based Capital Allocation	ERM provides a process in which capital is allocated considering the risks associated with the investment. Capital investments are pursued on a prioritized portfolio basis, thereby ensuring capital is allocated in the highest priority areas.	CEO, Executive Management, Business Unit Leaders
8th	Risk-Informed Business Decisions	ERM helps the organization's managers make daily business decisions based on relevant, timely, actionable, and reliable risk information using flexible risk management processes and tools.	Business Unit Leaders, Managers, Functional Heads
9th	Achievement of the Organization's Business Unit Goals	ERM increases the probability of achieving the organization's business unit goals by identifying key business risks and resolving contributing factors currently hindering the organization's ability to achieve the business goals.	Business Unit Leaders, Managers, Functional Heads
10th	Cost Savings	ERM clarifies cost savings and improvement opportunities through execution of risk management plans addressing contributing factors and key root causes such as redundancies, inefficiencies, and waste.	Business Unit Leaders, Managers, Functional Heads

Who Leads ERM?

Leaders with various educational and professional backgrounds may lead the ERM charge; however, most important to me is selecting a strong leader who has passion, persistence, and drive. Over the years, I have seen ERM work when championed by treasury, internal audit, strategic planning, risk management, legal compliance, and other departments. Keep in mind that the group that leads ERM tends to apply its own personal experience and bias. Therefore, ERM may "resemble" the group that designs and implements the approach.

Although ERM could, and probably should, be integrated with strategic planning, it does not mean ERM must be owned or facilitated by the strategic planning group. Just as one example, a *Fortune* 50 company successfully designed and implemented ERM through the treasury department for more than three years. Shortly after a new chief financial officer (CFO) decided to push ERM ownership over to strategic planning, it lost focus and momentum because the strategic planning leader had limited understanding of ERM and no passion for its success.

The ERM Framework

In this book, I spend considerable time discussing in detail the activities that pertain to each of the two approaches to ERM. While both approaches include activities that constitute a sizable portion of ERM, they are not intended to represent a complete ERM framework. To understand the full picture, the practical steps of ERM should be considered in the larger context of the ERM framework. Each approach's description begins with a depiction of its customized framework.

The purpose of an ERM framework is to help you, as an ERM champion or implementer, understand what components are necessary to help ERM "live and breathe" and continue to evolve within the company, whether or not you are still involved. In my experience, some ERM components frequently used include governance, infrastructure, integration, and foundation. These key components are necessary to sustain an effective risk management process, which includes steps such as risk assessment, risk analysis, action planning, and risk reporting and monitoring.

> Given that the framework is significant to sustaining ERM, it will probably seem counterintuitive when I suggest that you take care not to introduce it too early in your ERM activities. Why? I have found that when it is addressed too early, the ERM effort tends to get lost in philosophical discussions of each element of the framework itself instead of identifying and analyzing significant risks.

Gaining Commitment

To successfully initiate and implement ERM, you must get CEO buy-in and support. Other executives can certainly champion ERM for the organization, but ultimately CEO support is necessary to sustain value-add ERM.

> Here is one example of what real-world CEO support looks like. After completing an initial strategic risk assessment, the ERM team presented the top five residual risks to the seven-member executive team of a *Fortune* 200 railway company. One of those risks was summarized as "potential train derailment." I remember quite well the COO's initial response to that particular risk, "Derailment of trains is not a risk; that's our business!" Well, he was correct, in part. For this company, keeping trains on the track was clearly a key objective, necessary to generate revenue and continue as a business. And he, as COO, had the ultimate responsibility for ensuring that objective was met. However, he also had ultimate responsibility for making sure the risk of derailment was effectively managed, so his peers proactively provided additional insight into why it was a known risk of greater concern than in years past. They pointed out that the company's trains 1) carried hazardous materials, 2) through largely populated cities, and 3) had recently experienced some minor derailment incidents. Shortly thereafter, the CEO said, "This is a significant risk to our business, and you, COO, will bring an action plan for better managing this risk to me by next month." No more was said. No more needed to be said. That is what CEO support of ERM looks like.

Successful implementation of ERM, especially in the early stages, is more than getting buy-in; it also requires managing expectations. It is important to be very clear about what executives and management should expect from ERM. For example, I was often asked, "How do you do it and when is it done?" I frequently responded, "Here is how you do it, and there is no 'done.'"

This was probably not what they wanted to hear, but it was the truth. Remember, many executives are unlikely to know what ERM is all about; they are looking to you for that. I recommend you focus your communication with them on how ERM can help the organization. Explain how identifying and better managing key risks will help the company achieve strategic objectives and corporate goals, as well as the ERM objectives illustrated in **exhibit 1.1**.

Plain Speaking—Common Language

It is important to keep ERM simple and limit risk jargon as much as possible. Each profession tends to have its own lingo, and using it sometimes signifies that you are a "member of the club." That is undoubtedly helpful in some situations but not much in ERM, which is most successful when it receives support of management at all levels. Earning that support requires using language that resonates across multiple job titles and levels of responsibility. Using risk specialist jargon can be counterproductive and may alienate employees who have tremendous insight into risks—risks you need to know about.

As you go through the chapters in this book, you will see that we often talk about the importance of using a common language. It is difficult to make progress when every person in a meeting has a different understanding of the topic being discussed. Because executives have often worked in several different companies, they have probably run into different approaches to risk management over time. Chances are good that those approaches used their own language and definitions—reason enough to ensure everyone understands exactly what *you* mean when you talk about risk and ERM.

> I recall one CFO of a *Fortune* 150 retail company who said, "When risk happens, we are insured." I knew immediately that this CFO was not ready to embrace the breadth of ERM and its potential to identify and effectively manage a significant risk *before* it becomes a catastrophic event.

Common ERM Pitfalls

No business practice results in benefits without facing some potential pitfalls along the way. It is important to be aware of what challenges may lie ahead. Here are the most common pitfalls I have seen companies fall into while trying to introduce and evolve ERM:

- Lack of visible, active support from the CEO
- Trying to implement ERM without a framework and a strategic plan
- Overselling ERM's value, especially during early implementation
- Confusing risk assessment with ERM
- Treating ERM as a project rather than a long-term commitment
- Failing to carry risk management through the entire process
- Failing to realize the need for change management
- Failing to truly integrate ERM into key processes such as strategic planning, capital allocation, and budgeting

Probably one of the most common pitfalls is assigning ERM to the wrong champion. My experience indicates that when ERM fails, it is generally not due to the inadequacy of the activities but of the ERM team itself. Lack of passion or appreciation for all the soft skills necessary to lead ERM trumps even the most proven ERM tools and techniques. So, once you get the support of your executives, it is up to you to execute your plan. The rest of this book will help you do exactly that, so let's get to work.

CHAPTER 2

MANAGEMENT-VALUE APPROACH: STRATEGIC RISK ASSESSMENT

This chapter introduces the ERM framework for the management-value approach, discusses the framework's elements, and describes the activities involved in step 1 (risk assessment) of the risk management process.

As noted in chapter 1, this book covers two approaches. We begin with the management-value approach (discussed in this chapter and the next), which:

- Tends to be championed by executive management for the primary purpose of creating business value and a secondary purpose of helping the board fulfill its risk oversight role.

- Generally emphasizes the need to drive value through the identification and resolution of significant residual risks that could hinder the achievement of objectives and goals communicated to shareholders and other stakeholders.

- Makes it a priority to address the following common ERM objectives (see **exhibit 1.1**): risk-informed strategic decisions, achievement of organization's strategic objectives, and risk-based capital allocation.

Before we get into the risk management steps, it is important to understand how those steps align within a customized ERM framework. Remember, just as there is no "one right" approach to ERM, there is no "one right" framework. The framework I describe in this chapter has been used successfully with the management-value approach across companies and industries. Although you can use COSO ERM, ISO 31000, and other frameworks as a starting point, the key is to determine what is best for your management team and corporate culture, and tailor your ERM activities as needed.

ERM Framework

Take a look at the framework (see **exhibit 2.1**) and I will provide an overview of each element.

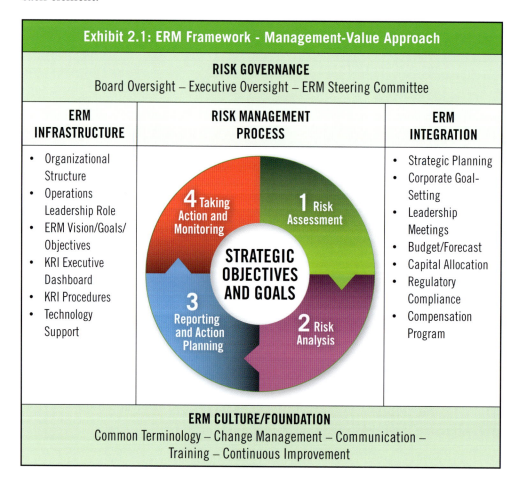

Risk Management Process

Let's start in the center with the risk management process, which has strategic objectives and goals at its core. The risk management process includes four steps: risk assessment, risk analysis, reporting and action planning, and taking action and monitoring. The use of the endless arrows reflects the ongoing, iterative nature of ERM.

Risk Governance

Risk governance is identified at the top. During the early stages of ERM implementation, a company may choose to have an ERM steering committee (mostly executive vice presidents [EVPs] and VPs providing overarching direction) and/or an ERM working group (management level tasked with getting things done). Some companies may even have a risk committee at the board level that helps with risk management oversight. Although some type of ERM committee is ultimately needed, I would caution against trying to initiate ERM through a committee structure. Relying on a committee during the early stages of ERM has generally proven to hinder timely progress due to limited knowledge of ERM and too many differing views on what effective risk management looks like.

ERM Integration

On the right side of the framework is ERM integration. This is where the framework states that ERM activities should ultimately be built into core company processes such as strategic planning, corporate goal setting, budgeting, capital allocation, and compensation program. However, you should not expect to immediately integrate ERM into all or, for that matter, any of your company's current processes. Typically, companies initiate ERM in stages to gain understanding of ERM and demonstrate value it can produce. Once that understanding has been developed, you can start identifying which business processes should be integrated with ERM for your company.

ERM Infrastructure

Supporting the risk management process (on the left side) is the infrastructure. A typical, often-debated question relating to infrastructure is whether or not a company must have a CRO. Do not become too concerned with ERM infrastructure too early in the implementation. Identifying a respected, passionate leader who truly understands and appreciates ERM and is in a position to speak to and be heard by the appropriate levels of authority in the organization is more important than the person's title. Ultimately, management will need to decide on the best ERM structure, ERM objectives, and technology necessary to support ERM for your company.

ERM Culture/Foundation

Across the bottom are the foundational elements that must be in place to support ERM. As already mentioned, common terminology is critical to the long-term success of ERM. Additional components such as change management and communication are important as well, especially during the early phases of implementation.

> Company culture can have a significant impact on the execution of ERM. For example, I was leading a meeting with the CEO of a *Fortune 1,000* company and his executive team to discuss a prioritized list of risks. For the most part, the CEO was expressing his views on the risks while the executives were generally silent. About halfway into the meeting, the CEO had to step out for another commitment. Shortly after he left, one of the remaining executives said, "Now that he's gone, we can really tell the truth." While this comment was met with laughter, it was clear that it carried a serious undertone. And, in fact, the conversation did start flowing more freely and candidly. If a company has a culture that does not support open and honest communication, especially between the CEO and direct reports, it is not healthy and certainly not helpful for ERM.

As I mentioned in chapter 1, becoming overly focused on the ERM framework early in your implementation can hinder progress on implementing ERM. I will tell you that management's eyes would sometimes glaze over as we attempted to inform them about the overall ERM framework. In fact, after that part of our discussion, management's first question was usually, "Now, what are you really going to do?" The second most common question was, "How do you expect to involve our employees?"

After years of trial and error, my experience clearly indicates that focusing on the execution of the risk management process is more productive than engaging in debates on all the surrounding framework components necessary to sustain ERM. Most every executive I worked with seemed to be far more interested in learning how we would help them identify the biggest risks to the achievement of their objectives versus installing a complete ERM framework.

Let's take a closer look at the risk management process in **exhibit 2.2**.

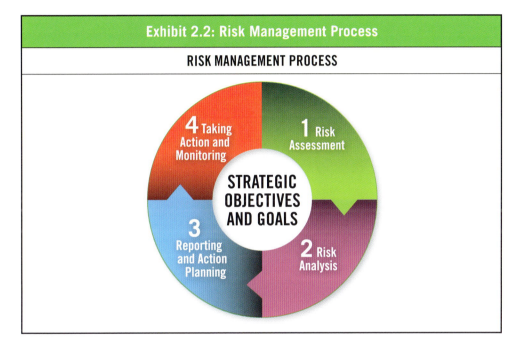

It is critical to remember that the first step—risk assessment—must get to the most significant risks to the achievement of your company's strategic objectives, just as illustrated in the ERM framework. One way this focus can be accomplished is by referring to your company's most recent strategic plan, including key corporate objectives. Most every company has a set of key objectives, even if they are less officially defined.

Risk Management Process Step 1: Risk Assessment

As the initial step of the risk management process, here is where you must effectively identify the top risks that matter most to management. Although there are many approaches to identifying and assessing risks, I have found the following approach (illustrated by the timeline in **exhibit 2.3**) to be quite effective and efficient. The timeline is depicted at a high level; supporting each of these major activities are far more detailed tasks.

Exhibit 2.3: Timeline for Risk Management Process Step 1: Risk Assessment			
Step 1 Activities	Month 1	Month 2	Month 3
Activity A: Preparation	➡		
Activity B: Conduct Interviews with Senior Management		➡	
Activity C: Compile, Review, and Summarize Risk Information			➡
Activity D: Present Key Risks to Executive Management Team and Select Top Risks for Detailed Risk Analysis			➡

Preparation (Activity A in the Timeline)

Preparation for the risk assessment is very important. Many times, I have reminded our team that we must "start with the end in mind." Once we have a good idea what our deliverable will look like, we can then make sure that we include all the necessary activities to get to that desired end product.

As part of your preparation, you need to select or develop an enterprise risk inventory, which is a comprehensive list of high-level, broadly defined risk inherent to the business across all categories of risk such as strategic, operational, legal, and financial. There are now plenty of versions of inventories to choose from. At this stage of ERM, the inventory can be somewhat generic and relevant for many different companies across industries. Although we offered customization of the inventory, most executives were fine with the general version we brought to the table during early stages of ERM implementation. I have used many versions of enterprise risk inventories over the years. **Exhibit 2.4** illustrates a fairly common one. Each risk is typically supported by a one-sentence risk definition, which is written in the form of a potential event.

Conduct Interviews with Senior Management (Activity B in the Timeline)

First, I want to say that I have tried many different approaches to identifying and assessing risks, including conducting thousands of one-on-one interviews, facilitating hundreds of workshops with groups of 12 to 15 employees, and sending surveys to employees at various levels. However, the most efficient and effective approach involves senior management through an interview process.

> Although the risk assessment approach I chose to illustrate in this book focuses on management interviews, I will stand by the additional value and insight you can gain by adding a few key workshops with leaders and subject matter experts (SMEs) who are a little deeper into the organization. When time allowed, we typically facilitated three to five workshops with 12 to 15 employees in each to gain their perspectives on the company's most significant risks. Most every workshop we facilitated resulted in very open and honest discussion by employees who truly cared about their company's success. Obtaining this insight, along with conducting interviews with the top executives, can provide even richer data from your initial step. So, risk assessment workshops, well facilitated, are yet another proven ERM activity used to "get to the truth."

Exhibit 2.4: Example Enterprise Risk Inventory for the Management-Driven Approach

External	Strategic	Operational					Financial
		Process	Information	Human Resources	Ethics	Technology	
• Capital Availability • Competition • Customer Needs • Economy • Financial Markets • Industry • Legal/ Regulatory • Natural Hazards/ Catastrophes • Political Environment • Shareholder Relations • Social Responsibility • Terrorism	• Brand • Business Model • Business Portfolio • Organizational Structure • Resource Allocation • Strategic Planning	• Business Interruption • Change Response • Compliance • Efficiency • EHS • Knowledge Management • Measurement • Product Development • Pricing • Supply Chain • Strategy Implementation • Transaction Processing	• Accounting Information • Budgeting/ Forecasting • Completeness/ Accuracy • Regulatory/ Reporting • Tax Reporting	• Accountability • Communications • Compensation • Competencies/ Skills • Empowerment • Legal • Recruiting/ Retention • Succession Planning • Training	• Conflict of Interest • Fraud • Illegal Acts • Third-Party Fraud	• Access • Availability • Capacity • Confidentiality • Data Security • Infrastructure • Innovation • Reliability	• Cash Flow • Credit • Equity • Foreign Exchange • Interest Rate • Liquidity • Reporting

Management-Value Approach: Strategic Risk Assessment

Before starting the risk assessment, it is critical to the success of ERM to gain visible, active support of the CEO. It is good practice for the ERM team leader to meet with the CEO early into the risk assessment to ensure understanding of the effort and support of ERM.

After gaining CEO support, the next step is to identify the individuals to involve in the interviews. I recommend targeting the group your organization recognizes as the "executive team," including some of their direct reports. Based on my experience, some of the appropriate titles might include EVP, senior VP (SVP), and VPs across all parts of the organization. The number of individuals in this group will vary depending on the size of the company, but it generally includes around 15 to 25 people. It is advisable to keep this group reasonably small while still involving the necessary leaders to represent good coverage of the company. A good question to ask the CEO is, "How many of your leaders do you need to hear from to believe the results and take action as needed?"

We typically conduct a one-hour interview with each of the individuals identified in the preceding paragraph, which is why I suggest keeping the group relatively small. To ensure no interviews are overlooked, we have found it quite helpful to set up a detailed spreadsheet indicating when each interview is scheduled and when it is completed. The goal is to hold the interviews in as short a time as possible—for example, 20 interviews over a two-week period—to keep the project moving and to be able to share results soon after all the interviews are completed.

> Both ERM approaches I am describing in this book rely heavily on interviews. I strongly recommend that at least two members of the ERM team facilitate each interview, preferably one capturing notes on a computer. It will help with remembering/recreating the discussion later. Effectively capturing the discussion is as important, if not more so, as facilitating the discussion. Your summary of results will only be as good as your interview notes.
>
> Why am I such a proponent of using interviews versus surveys to gather risk information? I am convinced that conducting one-on-one discussions, with the ERM team asking the right questions, enables getting to the truth at a depth that cannot be matched through a

> survey. The interview provides ample opportunity for the executive to share points of view within one hour.

Before scheduling the first interview, it is extremely helpful for the CEO to demonstrate support of ERM by sending a memo to the interviewees advising that they will be contacted to schedule an interview, describing the purpose of the interview, and notifying that some pre-read material will be coming for their review before their interview. Receiving this message from the CEO makes the importance of ERM very clear and sets an expectation for full participation by all involved.

The pre-read package should be provided to all interviewees a week or so before their interview and include the following:

- The enterprise risk inventory
- A brief definition of each of the risks
- The interview question and worksheet (see **exhibit 2.5**)

As you can see in **exhibit 2.5**, this template is quite simple, which is exactly what we intended to accomplish. The question is included at the top of the page so the interviewees can begin thinking about it in advance, even jotting down their ideas on the worksheet. Over the years, most executives completely filled out the template before the interview; some preferred handwritten notes while others typed. This worksheet can be used as an effective discussion source in the interviews.

I commonly request five risks; others may prefer only three. The exact number is not as important as selecting what works best for ERM at your company. Even so, I suggest that you keep it to a fairly small number. This tends to elicit the risks that are truly at the top of the interviewees' minds. If they feel they have to list, say, 10 risks, they are likely to start naming risks that are not truly of much concern to them, simply for the purpose of coming up with the requested number. Also, once you obtain the "top five risks" from about 20 executives, I assure you that you will end up with far more than five risks for the company, even after summarizing and consolidating the results.

Exhibit 2.5: Pre-Read Worksheet

Risk is defined as any potential activity or event that could have a negative impact on the achievement of objectives over the next three years, which is aligned with our strategic planning process. After reviewing the enterprise risk inventory and using your own experience, identify and summarize the five most critical risks.

Summary of Top Five Key Risks

1.

2.

3.

4.

5.

After sufficient planning, it is time to conduct the interviews. As a member of the ERM team, your goal is to encourage the interviewees to think beyond their specific business area; that is why you preface your question with a reference to their experience and a reminder to consider the enterprisewide risks, using those highlighted in the enterprise risk inventory as a reference. However, you want to be sure they do not simply look at the enterprise risk inventory and pick out four or five "from the list." Keeping the participant on track during an interview is not always effortless. To be most effective, you must keep the discussion on point and informative by asking probing questions. Sometimes, management has a tendency to summarize a risk in just a few short words. A good interviewer will drill deeper into a key risk to seek out driving factors, root causes, and risk management activities. Each interview will probably take about an hour and is likely to generate five to 10 pages of notes.

> In chapter 1, I noted that the management-value approach focuses on residual risks, whereas the board-confidence approach initially focuses on risks inherent to the business. You may have noticed that the preceding paragraphs include no mention of the ERM team pressing the interviewee to focus on residual risks. My experience is that making a special point of this is not necessary; it happens somewhat naturally. Generally speaking, the board tends to think in terms of inherent risk (any risk before considering risk management activities in place to manage the risk) and management naturally focuses on residual risk. It certainly doesn't hurt to specify "residual risks," but it is not essential to get good results.

Compile, Review, and Summarize the Risk Information (Activity C in the Timeline)

When you finish the interviews, you will have gathered a great deal of qualitative content (as much as 200 pages if you conduct 20 interviews), which is extremely rich and nuanced but not necessarily easy or speedy to consolidate. The ERM team will need to take ample time to parse through the comments to identify what rises to the top and why. There may even be a need for help from a strong team member who specializes in risk analysis, especially if the team conducted a large number of interviews.

What the team needs to produce at the end of the analysis is a strong list of the top eight to 15 risks. To do that, you will need to identify differently worded statements that ultimately refer to the same high-level risks. For example, one interviewee may mention a concern about explosions at an offsite location, another may refer to areas within the headquarters facility that present potential danger to employees and guests, and yet another may note an issue about the security of employees traveling to certain parts of the world. While these are three different situations, they all deal with safety, so your team may choose to combine them in a high-level risk titled "Employee Safety." Summarized below is a small sample of top-five risks highlighted for real companies over the years:

- **Core Customers**—Potential overdependence on core customers
- **Competitive Advantage**—Risk of losing our competitive advantage
- **Vendor Overreliance**—Potential overreliance on key vendors
- **Train Derailment**—Risk of train derailment, carrying hazardous materials
- **Business Interruption**—Potential inability to effectively sustain operations during a hurricane
- **Mechanical Failure**—Risk of mechanical failure causing an explosion or spill
- **Aging Leadership**—Potential inability to replace aging leadership
- **Acquisition Integration**—Potential ineffective integration of acquisitions

As one option, you can perform a light prioritization of the pre-compiled list based on the number of times a particular risk was mentioned in the interviews. For example, if you spoke with 20 individuals and 14 of them mentioned some aspect relating to safety, that risk would likely be at or near the top of the list. For step 1, the prioritization does not have to be any more scientifically calculated than this; it is just a quick means to identify certain themes that arise multiple times. An example report (generally presented in PowerPoint) summarizing the key risks is shown in **exhibit 2.6**. Whereas the exhibit shows only the slide for the first risk listed in slide 1, the actual report would include a separate slide for each of the four risks identified.

Practical Enterprise Risk Management: Getting to the Truth

Exhibit 2.6: Summary of Key Risks
Slide 1

Summary of Results

The following key strategic risks were identified during the 20 interviews with senior management:

A. **Acquisition Integration**—Potential ineffective integration of a strategic acquisition

B. **Financial Reporting**—Potential material misstatement of consolidated financial results

C. **Leadership**—Potential inability to replace key leaders due to aging population

D. **Competitive Advantage**—Potential inability to maintain competitive advantage

Slide 2

A. Acquisition Integration

Risk definition: Potential ineffective integration of a strategic acquisition

Risk Category					
External			Acquisitions		
Percentage of Interviews					
Risk Discussed	<20%	<40%	<60%	<80%	<100%

Key Contributing Factors:

- Limited acquisition experience among leadership team
- Significant cultural differences among acquired companies
- Inadequate IT infrastructure to support acquisition integration
- History of decentralized, autonomous operations
- Limited availability of qualified personnel to ensure successful integration

Present Key Risks to Executive Management Team and Select Top Risks for Detailed Risk Analysis (Activity D on the Timeline)

Once you have your list, it is time to convene with the CEO and EVPs (usually five to seven executives for an hour or so). In the meeting, explain that your analysis revealed these to be the top risks of concern and ask them which one(s) they want to be the subject of the strategic risk analysis to occur as the next step. Some companies choose only one from the list—and not necessarily the top one—and others choose to do a few or possibly all. Based upon my experience, three or four risks tends to be a reasonable number to manage in the strategic risk analysis (step 2), especially if you are in the early stages of ERM. Remember, when done right, these big risks will be critical to management and influencing the strategic direction of the company.

> For years we conducted a prioritization workshop with the top 12 to 15 leaders, primarily rating impact and likelihood to develop a risk map. This approach usually proved to be of value, but it had some flaws. First, the workshop would take three or four hours of the executives' time. Second, leaders tended to debate the voting results because much of the information was still at a high level and somewhat incomplete. Remember, these initial results came from conducting 15 to 20 one-hour interviews that were all independent of each other. Even for companies where we added four or five workshops and surveyed hundreds of employees, the information still had only so much depth.

During the early years of ERM, some companies got delayed after the initial strategic risk assessment (step 1). Management would like what had been done and agreed that the information needed to be considered during strategic planning efforts—and did so, to some degree. They did not, however, always recognize the need for ERM to be ongoing and ultimately become integrated with the strategic planning process or other core business processes over time. They interpreted the initial risk assessment step as ERM being "done." Instead, they should have thought in terms of, "Now we have started."

Why did that tendency occur? Perhaps it is because step 1 usually did not surface shocking results from the interviews. Most executives already have a good idea of what risks exist, so, while there may be a few "aha" moments, there are seldom "I never would have thought of that" revelations. In fact, I started telling management not to expect surprising results during the initial strategic risk assessment (step 1).

These reasons drove my team and me to develop activities for steps 2 and 3—strategic risk analysis and action planning (discussed in the next chapter)—and we emphasized with clients the need for those steps before beginning step 1. I continue to believe it is critical to get your company to steps 2 and 3 as soon as possible to truly demonstrate the potential of ERM.

A Summary of Steps and Outputs Discussed in This Chapter

Steps

1. Select an enterprise risk inventory.
2. Develop a timeline for the strategic risk assessment, which is step 1 of the risk management process.
3. Meet with the CEO to gain commitment for ERM.
4. Identify the leaders to be interviewed and schedule a one-hour interview with each.
5. Request the CEO demonstrate support of ERM by sending a memo to the interviewees about the upcoming interviews.
6. Develop the concise pre-read package and distribute it to the interviewees.
7. Conduct the interviews.
8. Compile, review, and summarize the comments gathered during the interviews and develop a consensus list of the top risks. Perform a light prioritization, if desired.
9. Present key risks to the CEO and EVPs and ask them to select the risks to be addressed in the next step.

Outputs

- A general enterprise risk inventory that serves an initial purpose for ERM
- A timeline for the strategic risk assessment (step 1)
- Pre-read material that poses the interview question and describes the elements of the enterprise risk inventory
- An assessment of the interview comments that reveals the top risks
- A selection of the risks to be addressed in step 2 (strategic risk analysis)

CHAPTER 3

MANAGEMENT-VALUE APPROACH: STRATEGIC RISK ANALYSIS AND ACTION PLANNING

This chapter describes the activities involved in step 2 (risk analysis), step 3 (reporting and action planning), and step 4 (taking action and monitoring) of the risk management process. It concludes with experience-based observations of the ERM framework elements surrounding the risk management process.

First, I must emphasize how important risk analysis and action planning—steps 2 and 3 of the risk management process (see **exhibit 2.2**)—are for ERM. In fact, without "real action," I think ERM fails. The approach to these steps described in this chapter has proven time and time again to add tremendous value to management and the company. As a reminder, we begin the strategic risk analysis with the output from step 1, risk assessment.

Risk Management Process Step 2: Risk Analysis

While many companies' management team truly have appreciated the results coming out of risk assessment (step 1) and usually took meaningful action on some of the information, the (intentionally limited) work done in step 1 generally struggled to consistently lead management to a productive strategic risk analysis (step 2) and meaningful reporting and action planning (step 3), which are critical for sustaining ERM. As I mentioned in the previous chapter, after expe-

riencing this "lesson learned" for a number of years, my team and I began making it clear from the start of ERM that step 2 (followed by step 3) is essential for ERM to start demonstrating more value. Although the risk assessment is a very good first step, the value is limited without proceeding to a deeper strategic risk analysis of the most significant risks. A timeline for the step 2 and 3 activities is depicted in **exhibit 3.1**.

> Similar to the risk assessment timeline (see **exhibit 2.3**), this timeline is also highly simplified. Each activity shown is the combined result of many smaller steps. My team and I generally set up a spreadsheet to list and track progress on those steps to ensure everything remained on track. Of course, you can use project management software as desired.

Project Planning (Activity A on the Timeline)

ERM will be only as successful as you make it. Like any significant initiative, effective and thorough planning is a must. It is best to "start with the end in mind." Although, at times, this has proven difficult with ERM, I continue to strongly encourage you to do your best to determine the preferred outcome from your project and develop all the necessary activities and associated timeline to achieve that desired outcome.

Exhibit 3.1: Timeline for Risk Management Process Step 2: Risk Analysis and Step 3: Reporting and Action Planning			
Step 2 and 3 Activities	Month 1	Month 2	Month 3
Activity A: Project Planning	██████▶		
Activity B: EVP Kickoff Meeting	▶		
Activity C: Risk Owner/Project Leader Kickoff Meeting		▶	
Activity D: Execute Risk Analysis With Risk Owners/Project Leaders		████▶	
Activity E: EVP Risk Vetting Session			▶
Activity F: Summarize and Communicate Risk Results to EVPs			▶
Activity G: Report Results to the Board/Audit Committee			▶

EVP Kickoff Meeting (Activity B on the Timeline)

An effective strategic risk analysis can take some meaningful time from management, so it is productive to conduct an executive kickoff meeting to discuss the upcoming activities and timeline. The primary purpose of the meeting is to ensure the executive team has a good understanding of the analysis activities, the time expected of them and their employees, and the deliverable. Once the executives realize the significance of the risk analysis, we ask them to identify the risk owners and team leaders for each risk be analyzed by the analysis team. These leaders (SMEs) will be responsible for completing the strategic risk analysis on their assigned risk from step 1.

This is probably a good place to emphasize the need for management to actively engage in the risk analysis (step 2) of ERM. As we know, risk is the responsibility of management. In fact, all employees across the company are responsible for managing risks to the achievement of objectives. ERM specialists, internal auditors, and risk managers can be a great resource to help management better understand risks and support the development of action plans to address risks as needed. Hence, step 2 is specifically designed with the intent of management committing meaningful time to execute the strategic risk analysis activities with the ERM team's oversight.

Over the years, it was quite common for me to hear risk managers, internal auditors, and others say, "Management does not have a lot of time to participate in 'our meetings.'" I would respond and emphasize the fact that these risk analysis meetings are necessary to adequately address the most significant risks that management believes can significantly impact the achievement of key objectives, perhaps even collapse the organization. Management meets all the time for topics most important to them. If your step 1, risk assessment, actually surfaces the most significant risks, management will make the necessary time to analyze those risks.

Risk Owner and Project Leader Kickoff Meetings (Activity C on the Timeline)

After the EVP kickoff meeting, the ERM team conducts another kickoff meeting, this one with all the risk owners and project leaders. Similar to the EVP kickoff meeting, the goal of this meeting is to ensure a solid understanding of the project, activities, and deliverable.

Part of the agenda should include a walkthrough of the pre-read package. The pre-read package (also presented in slide form during the meeting) describes the objective for the activity and discusses the members of the strategic risk analysis team for each of the top key risks identified for analysis. It also includes the risk information gathered during the risk assessment, which includes the risk definition and contributing factors (as taken from the interview comments). Finally, it includes the template in which the strategic risk analysis results will ultimately be summarized (see **exhibit 3.2**).

The risk analysis/action planning summary template provides an abbreviated format of the actual analysis, which will be much more extensive and detailed.

> I want to emphasize the value this simple, yet very effective, template brings to a risk analysis. At one *Fortune* 150 company, a board member expressed his appreciation of hearing about different risks through the same lens (template). No matter what the risk, he would hear the risk owner discuss the risk definition, risk scope, contributing factors, risk management activities, and action plans. The consistent reporting format allowed board members to focus on the risk content versus trying to understand the process or slant management may be taking to communicate a risk.

As noted earlier, having the risk owners conduct the analysis is useful because it demonstrates risk ownership and elevates their understanding of how important ERM is to the business. As they perceive its relevance, they are more willing to invest their time. It is not a matter of the ERM team doing something *to* them or *for* them; it is them doing the work the CEO says they should be doing because their particular risk is critically important.

The risk owner and his or her analysis team will be undertaking the bulk of the analysis, so it is important to bring them up to speed quickly, explaining the risk(s) to be analyzed and the information they must provide to complete the analysis. The risk(s) being analyzed in step 2 were described in only high-level terms in the risk assessment (step 1). They need to be analyzed in greater detail—an analysis that will enable the organization to do something meaningful with the risks.

Exhibit 3.2: Risk Analysis/Action Planning Summary Template

Risk Title	Insert Text	Impact Analysis ($MM)	
Risk Definition	Insert Text	Residual	Insert #
		Target	Insert #
Risk Scope			
Insert Text			
Risk Analysis Responsibility			
Risk Owner	Analysis Team	ERM Support	
Insert Text	Insert Text	Insert Text	
Contributing Factors/Risk Drivers			
Insert Text			
Current Risk Management Activities			
Insert Text			
Risk Management Plans			
Existing Plans	New Plans		
Insert Text	Insert Text		
Responsibility for Action Plan Implementation	Start Date	End Date	
Insert Text	Insert Date	Insert Date	

Execute Risk Analysis with Risk Owners/Project Leaders (Activity D on the Timeline)

Soon after the risk owners and project leaders are up to speed on the process, they initiate the risk analysis with their team. Again, to demonstrate risk ownership, the risk owners should be asked to issue an invitation to their team to attend a meeting and explain the meeting's purpose (focusing only on the risk assigned to them). The ERM team simply supports the analysis team as needed.

As with other meetings, it is advisable to provide some pre-read material (which my team called a "strategic risk analysis/action planning toolkit") to prepare the meeting attendees. The toolkit consists of exact instructions on what material to review before beginning the analysis (actual definitions of the risk under analysis and its contributing factors, as gathered during the risk assessment interviews). The team members are provided two templates to use to capture their analysis: a risk analysis/action planning detail template (see **exhibit 3.3**) and the risk analysis/action planning summary template, already shown in **exhibit 3.2**. The project leader works closely with the ERM team to ensure proper documentation of the risk analysis. It is common for several draft versions of the risk analysis to be prepared before a final version is completed.

Exhibit 3.3: Strategic Risk Analysis/Action Planning Detail Template
Section 1: Risk Overview
Risk Title
[Insert text]
Risk Definition
[Insert text]
Risk Scope
[Insert text]
Section 2: Contributing Factors *(Risk Drivers, Issues, Root Causes, Historical Events)*
[Insert text]
Section 3: Current Risk Management Activities *(Initiatives, Policies/Procedures, Processes/Controls, Organization/People, Systems/Technology, Measurement/Reports)*
[Insert text]
Section 4: Impact Analysis
Residual Risk Impact Analysis
[Insert text]
Target Risk Impact Analysis
[Insert text]
Section 5: Risk Management Plans *(Including Responsibility, Estimated Start Date, and End Date)*
Existing Risk Management Plans
[Insert text]
New Risk Management Plans
[Insert text]

It is important to thoroughly describe the analysis material to the teams to ensure a complete and actionable analysis. The risk owner and his or her team document the detailed strategic risk analysis/action planning results in sentence/paragraph format according to the following instructions, which describe the topics in **exhibit 3.3**:

- **Section 1: Risk Overview**—Provide appropriate guidance and clarity with respect to the definition and scope of the risk. Generally, the scope will highlight areas/items included in the strategic risk analysis as well as some areas/items specifically excluded.

- **Section 2: Contributing Factors**—Refine, clarify, remove, and/or add contributing factors that affect either the potential impact and/or likelihood of the risk occurring. Contributing factors are current risk drivers, issues, root causes, and/or historical events actually driving the concern about the risk. Contributing factors can be identified through discussion, review of documentation, and/or other, more thorough efforts such as causal analysis, decision tree analysis, review of historical events, and additional research in the industry. Provide appropriate detail to ensure that an effective analysis can be performed to determine whether the risk management activities are adequate relative to the contributing factors driving the concern about the risk.

- **Section 3: Current Risk Management Activities**—Identify and document existing risk management activities that are currently in place to address the risk. This should include current initiatives related to the risk, relevant policies and procedures, management processes, controls, people, systems, reports, measurement tools, and training. Only current (not planned) risk management activities should be identified and discussed in this section. Provide appropriate detail to ensure that an effective analysis can be performed to determine whether the risk management activities are adequate, in place, and functioning relative to the nature of the risk.

> All risks of this magnitude are being managed to some degree. The SMEs on the analysis team must dig a little deeper into the risk management activities to determine their true effectiveness. In my experience with multiple teams across companies, they all did just that. This held true for their work on continuing factors as well.

- **Section 4: Impact Analysis**—After completing sections 1 through 3, determine the estimated residual and target impact if the risk occurs. The level of sophistication and effort used to quantify the risk is subject to the risk type and technical capability of the analysis team. For residual risk impact, take into consideration the current risk management activities and determine the organization's residual exposure based on impact and likelihood. The residual risk impact may be greater or less than the risk sponsor's risk appetite and tolerance, so provide a target impact that would be considered more tolerable if the risk occurred.

  > More advanced ERM allows for more sophisticated risk measurement. Although some level of impact calculations can be applied on risks during step 1, risk assessment, more sophistication (i.e., risk quantification, risk modeling) can be applied during step 2 because you now have far more detailed information necessary for meaningful measurement and SMEs fully engaged in the process.

- **Section 5: Risk Management Plans**—Identify and document risk management plans as needed. Risk management plans may be needed if there are contributing factors that are not adequately managed and/or if there is a gap between residual risk impact and target risk impact. These plans may consist of two separate categories: "existing" and "new." Clarify and document existing risk management plans that are currently being considered to address the specific risk issue. In addition, document new risk management plans necessary to address the specific risk issue. Ultimately, the risk management plans should clearly identify the process that will be followed to develop an enhanced risk management approach to the risk. Provide appropriate detail, such as a cost-benefit analysis, to ensure that plans can be successfully implemented. Also indicate estimated start and end dates and the individuals responsible for the completion of the plans.

Once the entire document is complete, the risk owner and his or her team will summarize it in the risk analysis/action planning summary template previously provided (see **exhibit 3.2**) using bullet points.

Risk Management Process Step 3: Reporting and Action Planning

Risk Vetting Session (Activity E on the Timeline)

The risk vetting session is where the risk management process moves from step 2, risk analysis, into step 3, reporting and action planning. In practice, this line can be quite blurred. Once the risk material from each team is compiled, the results are communicated to the CEO and his or her direct reports (approximately eight to 12 people) for a two- to four-hour vetting session, depending upon the number of risks analyzed. It is important that this vetting session be run like an executive meeting. Therefore, transferring the risk analysis summary to slides that are used during the meeting can help keep the focus on the risk content and ensure consistency among the multiple risks presented.

During the meeting, each risk owner presents (in about 10 minutes) the conclusions and insights they developed while completing their analysis and their resulting risk management plans. This is followed by 10 to 15 minutes of questions, answers, and discussion.

This risk vetting session tends to be extremely effective. The results are communicated in an executive manner, one risk owner after another. Risk management plans are discussed, placing focus on what will occur or change as a result of the strategic risk analysis. The environment is one of trust because the participants sharing the risk analysis results are known experts with a strong

> I recall participating in one of these vetting sessions, and as the CEO left, he told me, "This was the best management meeting we have ever had." Note that he did not say "best *risk* meeting." Best *management* meeting. That indicates how very important, effective, and impactful this meeting can be.

business acumen. If these individuals indicate there is an area of concern, there *is* an area of concern. Some risk owners may have long known the risks, but the rigor of the risk analysis typically deepens their understanding of both the upside and downside of those risks.

> This workshop-type meeting, like any other, stands or falls on the abilities of the facilitator. How do you know if someone is a skilled facilitator? I have led and participated in many facilitated meetings, both good and bad. In my view, a good facilitator is almost forgotten during a workshop discussion. The best, most truthful information is offered when the participants are not talking to the facilitator; they are talking to, even debating, each other. A skilled facilitator makes that happen, then fades into the background until needed by the participants to keep the discussion productive and on point.

Summarize and Communicate Risk Results to EVPs (Activity F)

After the vetting session, it is time to circle back to the executive team with the final results. Upon further consideration of the risk analysis results, the executive team decides which risks need priority attention and action. At this point, they can create project plans, which can transition from words on a page to approved strategic plans, major projects, approved capital allocations, approved goals, and more.

> This is when risk assessment and risk analysis truly become part of the strategic direction of the company and help management better achieve objectives that are most important to key stakeholders.

Present Results to the Board/Audit Committee (Activity G on the Timeline)

There are many ways to communicate the results of a strategic risk analysis, as well as the initial results of the strategic risk assessment. For now, let's remain focused on communicating the risk analysis results to the audit committee and board. From my point of view, one of the most effective processes for reporting the risk analysis results was done at a *Fortune* 50 company.

First, because the CEO clearly recognized the breadth of the risks included in the risk analysis, he chose to communicate the risks to the full board, not just the audit committee. To again emphasize management ownership of risks, the executive-level risk owners personally presented the results using the same template (via slides) that they used for the vetting session. For this company, as a start, two of the top 12 risks analyzed were presented to the entire board. They shared the slides for about 10 minutes and allowed 15 minutes or so for questions.

Risk Management Process Step 4: Taking Action and Monitoring

A passion of mine is seeing risk assessment and risk analysis results lead to meaningful action to better manage risk and better achieve objectives. I would rather surface two or three significant risks that management embraces than a laundry list of risks that, quite frankly, no one cares about except the risk specialists or internal auditors who are reporting the risks. Based on my experience, I have seen management take action on ERM results time and time again. Why? Because we provided "the right information, to the right people, at the right time."

No risk management process should end without some type of action being taken for risks causing an unacceptable level of exposure. For enterprise risk, action is certainly not easy to take. Many times, action plans take years to fully implement. Sometimes, the action plans drive strategic initiatives related to the company's long-term goals and objectives.

Regarding monitoring, chapter 8 expands on monitoring the performance and status of risk. The one point I want to make here is that monitoring by an independent internal audit or risk management group tends to be a little less necessary when you find risks that truly can impact company performance and achievement of objectives. Once the action plans become major projects or strategic initiatives, management tends to put in ample "monitoring" procedures to ensure successful execution.

What's Next: Other ERM Components

With all the activity that has been undertaken in this chapter and the previous chapter, some management teams may believe they have "done" ERM by this point. That conclusion would be wrong. They have only gone around the risk management process for the first time. Let's revisit the ERM framework (see **exhibit 3.4**).

Now that you have designed and successfully executed your risk management process, it is time to focus on the other four ERM components. However, beyond the risk management process, practical application of ERM becomes more difficult to figure out and requires even more customization to meet management needs and the corporate culture.

Since I have already provided a summary of the ERM framework components in chapter 2, in this section I will primarily highlight some key points and lessons learned relative to the components that surround the risk management process. Remember, the goal is to build the right ERM framework for your company that contains the components necessary to sustain ERM, add value, and protect that value. Avoid getting caught up in the "ideal" and "should be's" that you may hear from ERM gurus or consultants. It is certainly fine to seriously consider all that ERM offers, but you must customize and apply the ERM tools and techniques that fit your management needs and company culture.

Here are a few observations from my experience working with ERM frameworks.

Risk Governance

The board oversight role tends to vary across industries and companies. A big decision point is whether the company needs a board-level risk committee, an executive-level risk committee, or both. Once that is determined, I recommend using an existing committee that is already established, if possible.

In the early stages of ERM development, implementation, and evolution, it usually is best to have an ERM steering committee to demonstrate cross-functional leadership support of ERM and provide guidance to ensure the approach is aligned with the company's business model and culture. A word of caution: avoid getting too involved in the risk governance component until you, your executives, and your board have a solid understanding of ERM.

> This affirms that ERM is supposed to be integrated into the fabric of your company, not "built on top of everything else."

ERM Integration

This component can be challenging. Most ERM guidance strongly suggests integrating ERM into strategic planning. Conceptually, I support that point of view, but I seldom saw it fully integrated in the real world, especially during the early stages of ERM. Once again, this varies quite a bit across industries.

One key point of clarification is that most companies initiating ERM do not immediately try to fully integrate it into strategic planning. Of course, you can link your initial risk assessment to the company's strategies and goals. I have seen ERM results fed into a strategic planning discussion and I have seen ERM results generated after the plan was developed to determine the significant risks to successful execution of the plan. Both worked well.

> One *Fortune* 500 manufacturing company had such tremendous results in step 1, risk assessment, that the executive team decided to fully integrate ERM into the company's business model, strategic planning process, capital allocation, performance management, etc., as their immediate next steps. They transferred one of their highly respected engineers to design and implement this fully integrated approach. Unfortunately, truly building ERM into every core strategic and business process that early into implementation proved to be very difficult. After making some progress over the next year, management expected more great results (i.e., more insightful risk information). The engineer was so busy "integrating ERM" that he had no time left to identify and communicate the risks that mattered. So, he went back to engineering, and ERM stalled for some time before getting renewed attention.
>
> That was an example of focusing on integration to the exclusion of other ERM activities. On the opposite end of the spectrum is an example of a different, yet still unsuccessful, outcome. A CFO at a *Fortune* 100 company wanted to demonstrate "seamless" ERM integration with the annual budgeting process. Unfortunately, the approach was so seamless it actually resulted in a 10-minute "check-the-box" approach that was nearly worthless. The lesson here is that if the ERM-related change to an existing core process is that minimal, you probably are not enhancing the process or integrating ERM.

ERM Infrastructure

The ERM infrastructure decision has been, and continues to be, a difficult one. CRO or not? House ERM in strategic planning, finance, legal, etc.? Internal audit to play a key role or a distant one? Keep ERM at the strategic level or up, down, and across the organization? These and many more questions will ultimately need to be answered for your company. Do not expect too much clear guidance on this component as it has generated much controversy this past 20 years and may continue for some time into the future. Ultimately, do what is best for your management team and corporate culture.

While policies and procedures are an important part of an ERM framework, be careful not to create too many too soon. I realize this will vary by industry, but it is important to minimize bureaucracy as much as possible.

I will discuss it in more detail in chapter 8, but I will mention here that an executive dashboard for key risk indicators as well as key performance indicators is potentially an excellent tool to support ERM, especially as a monitoring step.

ERM Foundation/Culture

The ERM foundation/culture component is the most important of all. It is referred to as the foundation for good reason. If you build it correctly, ERM will not only survive but thrive.

Although building an effective risk management process is of significant importance to ERM, do not underestimate the equally important need for a common language, effective change management, and clear communication, especially during the early stages of implementation. These elements must be done well to design, implement, and sustain effective ERM. Hence, the soft skills of the ERM leader far outweigh tools and techniques.

Clearly, there is a lot packed into the framework and we could spend many more pages discussing each element. Each element is important to sustain ERM and must be in place and functioning well, but if the risk management process (the center circle) is not done well, the surrounding framework elements are unlikely to be understood or seen as adding value.

It is for that reason this book places more emphasis on the practical application of the risk management process. This leads to the second approach to be covered in this book, the board-confidence approach, which uses a different risk management process to achieve different ERM objectives but with the same goals: identifying, assessing, understanding, and managing enterprise risk to the achievement of objectives.

A Summary of Steps and Outputs Discussed in This Chapter

Steps

1. Develop a timeline for steps 2 (strategic risk analysis) and 3 (action planning and reporting).
2. Develop and distribute to the executive kickoff meeting participants the pre-read package that will prepare them for the meeting.
3. Hold the executive kickoff meeting to discuss the material.
4. Develop and distribute the pre-read package to the participants of the risk owners' kickoff meeting.
5. Hold the risk owners' and project leaders' kickoff meetings to discuss the pre-read package.
6. Facilitate the process of the risk owners analyzing their assigned risk(s).
7. Forward the risk owners' analyses to the CEO and direct reports.
8. Facilitate a risk vetting session with the CEO and direct reports to vet the analyses.
9. Distribute the results of the vetting meeting to management and staff to incorporate into strategic plans and budgets.

Outputs

- A timeline for the strategic risk analysis (step 2) and reporting and action planning (step 3)
- A pre-read package for the executives' and risk owners'/project leaders' kickoff meeting
- The risk owners' analyses of their risk(s)
- Vetted analyses for use by management and staff

CHAPTER 4

BOARD-CONFIDENCE APPROACH: ENTERPRISE RISK INVENTORY

This chapter introduces the ERM framework for the board-confidence approach, discusses the framework's elements, and describes the initial activities involved in creating the enterprise risk inventory.

As mentioned in chapter 1, this book covers two approaches. (Remember, the titles used for the two approaches are primarily to help highlight the philosophical differences for the purpose of this book.) We have completed the management-value approach and will now begin the board-confidence approach (covered in this chapter and the next three), which:

- Tends to be championed by executive management for the primary purpose of helping the board fulfill its risk oversight role and a secondary purpose of creating business value.

- Generally focuses on gaining board comfort that management understands, communicates, and manages all significant risks to the organization.

- Makes it a higher priority to address the following common ERM objectives (see **exhibit 1.1**): board comfort and confidence, reduced reputational damage and operational surprises, and portfolio view of risks.

ERM Framework

As we did with the management-value approach, we will begin the board-confidence approach with an overview of a framework—this one significantly customized to the company. Compared to the management-value approach framework (see **exhibit 2.1**), this framework (see **exhibit 4.1**) is relatively simple, direct, and easy to understand. In fact, it was developed with a goal of leveraging as much of the existing company structure and resources as possible, as opposed to establishing new entities dedicated to ERM. The underlying principle for this customized framework is: ERM must be built into the fabric of the organization, recognizing and leveraging as much as possible the existing risk management that is already established and working well.

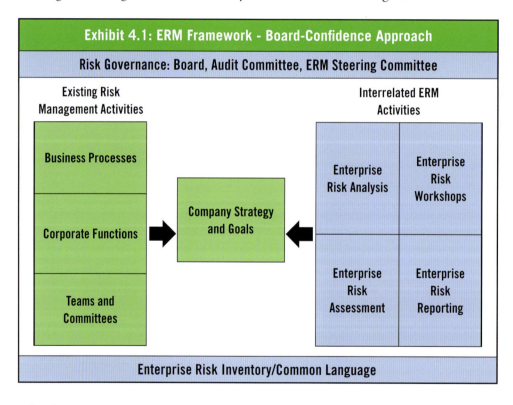

Like the management-value approach framework, company strategy and goals are at the center, emphasizing the need for ERM to remain focused on company goals, strategy, and objectives.

Risk Governance

At the top is the governance layer. Instead of creating a separate board-level risk committee, some companies I worked with used the existing audit committee, along with the full board, to play a key risk oversight role for ERM. Also, the executive management team chose to assume the responsibilities of an ERM steering committee with a twofold purpose: 1) steering the ERM efforts and 2) considering the significant risks that could impact strategic objectives. Again, each company must choose the best risk governance structure that is most appropriate for its own culture.

Existing Risk Management Activities

On the left side, feeding into (supporting) the strategy and goals, are the existing risk management activities (business processes, corporate functions, and teams and committees). These are common activities that tend to be in place to manage the business and address risk before and after ERM is implemented—processes such as engineering; environmental, health, and safety; procurement; corporate insurance; and legal compliance. They predate ERM and will go on even if ERM goes away. These activities represent, in my estimation, about 85 percent of what the company does every day to manage risk toward the achievement of objectives. They are reflected in the framework to emphasize the importance of continuing effective risk management activities that have helped, and will continue to help, the company succeed. As ERM champions, we must realize that management has been managing risks—most of the time, very well—and will continue to do so. Otherwise, far more companies would have already collapsed. With that said, I believe just about every organization can get better at managing risk. That is why ERM is still living and breathing today.

Interrelated ERM Activities

On the right side, also supporting company strategies and goals, are the four ERM activities that were developed to fill a risk management void at the enterprise level:

- Enterprise risk analysis
- Enterprise risk assessment
- Enterprise risk workshops
- Enterprise risk reporting

Enterprise Risk Analysis	Enterprise Risk Workshops
Enterprise Risk Assessment	Enterprise Risk Reporting

These activities are described in chapters 5, 6, and 7, including appropriate enterprise risk reporting for each ERM activity. It is important to understand that these activities have mostly been added to risk management rather than integrated into core processes. This fact drives much of the simplicity of the tools and techniques as well as the reason the activities are heavily reliant on the ERM team to execute.

Enterprise Risk Inventory/Common Language

Although other ERM foundational elements exist, the two most important are listed at the bottom of the framework: enterprise risk inventory and common language. These are the main foundational elements supporting ERM and communicated to management. However, change management, communication, and other traditional foundation elements certainly have a presence in this approach as well.

This framework was developed to serve several purposes: to be easily understandable, to address what management wanted, to demonstrate that significant risk management activity was already underway, and to introduce the four new ERM activities. The leaders of the company using this framework had no appetite for bureaucracy; they wanted a succinct and simple depiction of what ERM looked like within the company. The framework accomplished exactly those goals and was well received by management.

Customized Enterprise Risk Inventory

In chapter 2, we discussed the importance of the enterprise risk inventory for the management-value approach. It is even more important for the board-confidence approach. Simply stated, for ERM to be effective, the enterprise risk inventory should be the foundation for every other ERM component. Unlike the management-value approach, the board-confidence approach's enterprise risk inventory focuses on all critical inherent risks, fully customized for the company.

In my experience, board members naturally tend to think about risk through an inherent risk lens. They are generally independent of company management so they are more distant from all the tools, techniques, and people engaged in managing the company's risks every day, every hour. For example, let me take you to a *Fortune* 50 company, where board members, along with management, were individually asked to provide their top five risks to the company and its strategies. While management tended to name residual risks (risks after risk management activities have been considered) of great concern, board members tended to name risks inherent to the business. I recall one board member who listed ethics as the company's number one risk. Early into the discussion, however, he made it clear he did not believe management was unethical—in fact, quite the opposite. But he considered ethics so critical to the business and its reputation that he wanted to be confident that management also appreciated this particular risk and had the right processes in place to adequately manage it. By the way, this was not the only risk on top of the board's list that was not high on management's list. Providing insight on risks inherent to the industry and your company is simply one illustration of how board members can contribute to ERM while providing their primary role of risk oversight.

An indicator of an effective enterprise risk inventory is having a one-page summary of all significant risks expressed in common business terms typically used by your management (limited use of risk management and internal audit jargon). Of course, that means the risks have to be expressed in fairly high-level terms, which gives them room to stretch to generally represent all of your company's risks.

Identifying Risks for the Enterprise Risk Inventory

Of course, I do not recommend you start building the inventory by going to your board members—or management, for that matter—with a blank sheet of paper and asking them to start naming their top risks. Do some homework first.

The ERM team should get together, review the company's objectives and strategies, do some brainstorming, and develop a list of risks that seem appropriate and relevant for the enterprise risk inventory as a starting point. Once you have a general idea of what you want your inventory to look like in the end (targeting a list of between 15 and 20 broad enterprise risks grouped in four or five sections), you can consult some of the following sources other ERM leaders have used to research and further flesh out their risk inventory:

1. **Peers and consultants**. Peers and consultants may be willing to share their own risk inventories with you—at least the high-level enterprise risks.

2. **The personal experience of the ERM team members**. Chances are good that most members of the ERM team have been working in the company or industry for a number of years—long enough to have a good sense of the risks the organization faces.

3. **Risk specialists or internal auditors**. Risk managers across all disciplines and internal auditors have documented all sorts of risks that tend to arise as material concerns.

4. **The U.S. Securities and Exchange Commission (SEC) 10-K report**. U.S. federal securities laws mandate that certain companies file a 10-K annually. While it covers many topics, what is pertinent in an ERM context is Item 1A—Risk Factors, in which the filing company describes things that could go wrong, likely external effects, possible future failures to meet obligations, and any other risks that should be disclosed to adequately warn investors and potential investors.

5. **ERM frameworks and books**. ERM frameworks may contain helpful taxonomies, as may other ERM books covering the enterprise risk inventory topic.

6. **Employee surveys**. If your company has completed some type of risk survey (including surveys on ethics-related programs, regulatory compliance, and organizational culture) relatively recently, review the results to see what risks rose to the top. It is likely that many of those risks remain relevant to your organization and can provide useful information and insights.

After you and your team have gathered insightful material from these sources, the real work begins. You can start customizing risks to specifically reflect your company's operations, business terminology, and culture. The format illustrated in **exhibit 4.2** has worked very well for dozens of companies and includes 19 sample enterprise risks.

> In the management-value approach, the ERM team selects and slightly revises an inventory that aligns reasonably well with the company. Later, interviews are conducted and strategic risk documentation for significant residual risks is developed. You will see that in the board-confidence approach, interviews are conducted with risk sponsors, risk coordinators, and SMEs to identify the inherent risks in each enterprise risk and develop the documentation for each.

I must emphasize the point that this stage of developing a customized enterprise risk inventory is not a result of a risk assessment. This is simply identifying those enterprise risks that are of critical importance to achieving objectives and executing strategies, and protecting and enhancing company value.

Exhibit 4.2: Example Risk Inventory with Sample Enterprise Risks			
STRATEGIC			
Stakeholders	Strategy	Public Policy	Economy
OPERATIONS			
Procurement	Project Execution	Products	Market Capacity
Data Security	Portfolio	Environmental, Health, and Safety	Disasters
CORPORATE			
Human Resources		IT Systems	Regulatory
FINANCIAL			
Capital	Pricing	Financing	Financial Reporting

You will note throughout the book that my ERM team relied on manual processes and simple software rather than sophisticated software. Of course, we knew that sophisticated technology existed to support ERM activities; some organizations used it then, as they do now, but we consciously chose not to use it. Our philosophy was (and remains) that software should follow and support the process you design to serve the needs and accomplish the objectives of your company, not drive the process you use because it aligns with the software. Develop your process first; then if you can find and customize software to support it and make it more efficient, use it. My team, in collaboration with the IT department, looked into various software packages at times but never found a solution that provided enough value to us.

A Summary of Steps and Outputs Described in This Chapter

Steps

1. Brainstorm potential risks your company may face in achieving its objectives and executing strategies.
2. Do your research on risks more specific to your company.
3. Based on the research, customize a list of 15 to 20 enterprise risks.
4. Populate the enterprise risk inventory form with the enterprise risks.

Outputs

- An enterprise risk inventory that contains risks specific to the enterprise

CHAPTER 5

BOARD-CONFIDENCE APPROACH: ENTERPRISE RISK ANALYSIS

This chapter discusses creating definitions for the enterprise risks identified in the enterprise risk inventory, inserting the inherent risks in the enterprise risk inventory, and building the enterprise risk analysis (the inherent risk summary and the executive summary forms).

Once you have a preliminary list of 15 to 20 high-level risks, it is time to start the process of fully customizing the enterprise risk inventory by identifying the top two to four inherent risks within each enterprise risk. There is nothing magical about this number of inherent risks, but my experience indicates that most enterprise risks seem to be adequately defined by management using a few key inherent risks.

Enterprise Risk Analysis	Enterprise Risk Workshops
Enterprise Risk Assessment	Enterprise Risk Reporting

Below are some key steps you can follow to effectively populate the enterprise risk inventory.

Step 1. Draft a one-sentence risk definition for each enterprise risk.

Step 2. With the appropriate risk coordinators (usually SVP or VP level), identify/refine the inherent risks.

Step 3. Build the enterprise risk analysis.

Step 4. Roll inherent risk information up to the enterprise risk.

Step 1. Draft a one-sentence risk definition for each enterprise risk.

First, for each enterprise risk, write a brief definition—typically one sentence—describing what the potential risk event could be. This will undoubtedly be refined later, so do not belabor it at this point. Then, identify the highest-ranking nonexecutive in the company over that area of risk. In my experience, that person is typically at the SVP or VP level. In this book, this individual will be referred to as the risk coordinator, whereas the EVP will be referred to as the risk sponsor.

> Some ERM material refers to the EVP (risk sponsor) as the risk owner. One company I worked with consciously chose to use the term *risk sponsor* because the COO did not want to send the message to employees that only one person is responsible for a particular risk. He wanted employees to understand that every employee has some level of responsibility for helping the company manage all its risks. So, the risk sponsor and risk coordinator at this company primarily represented the go-to leaders for a particular risk. The point is, you need to use whatever term will be understood and accepted in your organization.

Step 2. With the appropriate risk coordinators, identify/refine the inherent risks.

Once you have identified the most likely risk sponsors and risk coordinators for your 15 to 20 enterprise risks, confirm the list with your executive team. It is not unusual for some names to change; your executives know best who the risk coordinators should be because they work with their leaders all the time.

Once the risk coordinators are confirmed, set up a one-hour meeting with each to explain why and how his or her particular enterprise risk was identified, how it fits into the enterprise risk inventory, and what role the inventory will play in the ERM. Then, share the draft definition of the risk and confirm that the definition is on the right track; it is not necessary to wordsmith it at this point, you just want to ensure the business leaders share the same general understanding of what the enterprise risk encompasses.

Next, ask the leader, "What are the most significant things that can go wrong in this area? What are the three or four big risks in your mind relative to this enterprise risk?" Be sure to prompt the risk coordinator to include new and emerging risks in his or her consideration. Try not to get too bogged down in typical risk management or internal audit jargon, such as inherent risk versus residual risk. Just keep the conversation simple and adjust to the business jargon that management uses to run the business. For example, an exploration and production company's COO defined one of the company's enterprise risks as "exploration." Hmm, I thought, I have never heard that one before. In one sense, that one enterprise risk represented half of the entire business. However, it was clearly how he and other executives thought about the "big risks that matter most." So, why shouldn't we ERM or risk specialists think the same way? Hopefully, that thought process makes sense to you.

As we talk with the risk coordinator about key inherent risks, ask what *could* happen, not whether it *will* happen. The resulting risks should not consider risk management activities (or controls) already in place. When my team and I did this, it usually took the full hour to have this discussion the first time around. It is a discussion you need to have with each risk coordinator of the remaining enterprise risks.

When you have finished these interviews, you can complete your one-page enterprise risk inventory sheet by listing the appropriate inherent risks under the appropriate enterprise risks (see **exhibit 5.1**).

Exhibit 5.1: Completed Example Enterprise Risk Inventory			
STRATEGIC			
Stakeholders	**Strategy**	**Public Policy**	**Economy**
• Core Customers • Investors • Community	• Strategy Development • Strategy Execution • Competition	• Public Policy • Political Climate	• National Economic Conditions • Global Economic Conditions
OPERATIONS			
Procurement	**Project Execution**	**Products**	**Market Capacity**
• Suppliers • Materials Management • Logistics	• Project Prioritization • Project Management	• Core Products • Product Management • Product Costs	• Capacity • Facilities
Data Security	**Portfolio**	**Environmental, Health, and Safety**	**Disasters**
• Data Governance • Data Quality • Data Classification	• Portfolio Strategy • Investment Decisions	• Health and Safety • Environmental Stewardship • EHS Compliance	• Natural Hazards • Terrorism • Explosion/Fire
CORPORATE			
Human Resources	**IT Systems**		**Regulatory**
• Recruitment • Retention • Employee Development • Work Environment	• IT Governance • Business Continuity • Information Security		• Regulation Awareness • Regulatory Compliance
FINANCIAL			
Capital	**Pricing**	**Financing**	**Financial Reporting**
• Capital Availability • Investment	• Price Strategy • Price Volatility	• Counterparty Credit • Credit Rate	• Information Accuracy • Financial Reporting

This enterprise risk inventory format looks similar to the one produced in the management-value approach (see **exhibit 2.4**) and contains similar components: sections, enterprise risks, and associated risks. The main difference is that this inventory is significantly more customized to the organization.

Step 3. Build the enterprise risk analysis.

As you progress on finalizing a solid enterprise risk inventory, you can begin to flesh out the enterprise risk analysis, keeping in mind that these activities are iterative and developments in one activity may necessitate revisions in the other.

Although I have seen this process applied at several companies over the years, one company in particular absolutely nailed this step. So, I am sharing that "best practice" approach (from my point of view) with you. You will need to complete one of these inherent risk summary forms for every inherent risk within the enterprise risks. For example, if you have 19 enterprise risks and an average of three inherent risks within each, you will complete 57 inherent risk summaries. This may sound like overkill and way too much granular detail, but I promise you that this step, which starts building your common language, actually gives more credibility to the company's big risks and keeps them at a higher level. You cannot arrive at a true common language without meaningful time and effort.

Please do not consider this busywork. It is a critical early step for building the foundation of ERM. The purpose of ERM is not to create a risk taxonomy that is so generic it can be used by about any organization. It is to understand the risks integral to achieving objectives and executing strategies, and assessing them so that gaps can be identified and appropriate action plans can be developed. My team and I developed the template illustrated in **exhibit 5.2** to capture the information we would need to take ERM to the next phase.

Completing the Inherent Risk Summary

To tackle the inherent risk summary form (see **exhibit 5.2**), you and your team will take the same approach you took to define the enterprise risks.

Exhibit 5.2: Inherent Risk Summary Form	
Section 1: Inherent Risk Overview	
Risk Name:	**Risk Sponsor:** (Name, title)
	Risk Coordinator: (Name, title)
Risk Definition:	
Risk Scope:	
Section 2: Contributing Factors	**Section 3: Risk Management Activities**
1. Insert numbered list, in order of importance.	1. Insert numbered list.
Section 4: Opportunities/Issues	
Insert opportunity/issue and description.	
Section 5: Risk Management Plans	
Insert risk management plans with brief descriptions.	

Based on the homework you have already done and some additional research you may opt to do, you will begin to fill out each section to the best of your ability based on what you already know and what you have learned, and then you will flesh it out through interviews with appropriate SMEs (risk coordinators and others). This is an iterative activity.

My team undertook the process of completing this form one inherent risk at a time. Based on the 48 risks we had to define, it required a six- to nine-month effort for three or four full-time-equivalent employees. Overall, this part of the process involved more than 100 people (SMEs) throughout the company.

In Section 1. Inherent Risk Overview, you already have the risk sponsor's and risk coordinator's names. For now, leave the definition and the scope boxes in general terms.

Then proceed to Section 2. Contributing Factors. What contributing factors drive that particular inherent risk? Some factors may be specific to the company, others may be environmental or industry-related, still others may arise from the competition, and some may be regulatory. It is likely that some of the contributing factors you identify will apply across a broader spectrum of business issues. For example, a contributing factor for a safety inherent risk for a drilling company could be, "Our employees operate daily in a highly dangerous environment." Another might be, "Our safety employees are decentralized, reporting to the local general manager who may have revenue targets that compete with safety targets."

Next, move on to Section 3. Risk Management Activities and define the risk management activities (i.e., controls, if you want to use some internal audit jargon) already in place. It is important to focus the entries in this section on activities already in place based upon the SME's perspective.

At this point, it is time for another discussion with the risk coordinator. Review the draft list of contributing factors and risk management activities with the risk coordinator for his or her particular enterprise risk. Ask the risk coordinator about the accuracy and relevance of the items captured on the form. Request suggestions for revisions or additions. Ask the risk coordinator if he or she recommends you talk to the pertinent managers and supervisors for additional insight to the enterprise risk.

Use the information you gather from these interviews to flesh out sections 2 and 3. Be sure to list the contributing factors in order of importance as best you can with the risk coordinator. This order doesn't have to be arrived at via formal survey or voting; general agreement is fine.

Now it is time to return to section 1. Based on the information now on the page, refine the draft risk definition and a risk scope. Getting these two entries right is likely to require more conversations with the risk coordinator, who will have a tendency to want to approve every word. The risk coordinator will pay special interest because he or she knows that ultimately this material will end up in the hands of at least the executive team, and probably the board. Be prepared to go through several drafts.

It is now time to discuss Section 4. Opportunities/Issues with the risk coordinator (this can be done after the definition and scope discussions). It is unlikely that there will be an entry in this section for every inherent risk because the items in this section represent serious gaps—places where there are inadequate risk management activities in place to address certain contributing factors, meaning a threat may become a reality. Having no entries in this section is a good thing. Even one can be considered too many. In my previous experience, we had 50 inherent risks, of which fewer than 10 had entries in section 4.

> Because the entries in section 4 are likely to be reviewed by the board, the company may have a preference as to how the information is conveyed. Some companies prefer to use fairly low-key, soft-edges language; others may want the information expressed in a very direct way. Corporate culture has a significant influence on issues such as this, consequently the approach to section 4 should be a strategic decision made by the company.

The information you provide in section 5, which you develop in collaboration with the risk coordinator and sponsor, is management's suggested action to help resolve or capitalize on the significant opportunities/issues noted in section 4, if any. A completed example is illustrated in **exhibit 5.3**.

Exhibit 5.3: Environmental, Health, and Safety Example
Inherent Risk Summary: Health and Safety

Section 1: Inherent Risk Overview

Risk Name: Health and Safety	**Risk Sponsor:** John Smith, EVP, Operations
	Risk Coordinator: Jane Doe, VP, EHS

Risk Definition: Potential failure to perform tasks safely and maintain the health of employees

Risk Scope: Includes all types of activities that may impact the health and safety of employees in all geographies

Section 2: Contributing Factors	Section 3: Risk Management Activities
1. High-risk activities	1. Company's EHS policy
2. Organizational change—new leaders	2. Monthly safety leadership team meetings
3. Operations completed by less experienced employees	3. EHS audits
	4. Executive commitment to safety
4. Accident reporting	5. Codes of practice
5. Safety culture	6. Mandatory safety training

Section 4: Opportunities/Issues

High-risk activities: It is the nature of the business for company employees to perform high-risk activities that could result in serious injuries and/or fatalities. The company has not recently evaluated the employees' safety performance.

Section 5: Risk Management Plans

High-risk activities: Develop health and safety academy training, requiring employees to complete the training on a yearly basis.

As you can see, much of the analysis in the board-confidence approach covers the same information that was discussed in chapter 3 for the management-value approach. However, there are differences:

- In the board-confidence approach, each inherent risk summary form covers only one inherent risk, and the information from all the inherent risks in a particular enterprise risk is rolled up into the executive summary. In the management-value approach, the information is gathered on a single strategic risk (identified at the end of risk management process step 1, strategic risk assessment).

- Another major difference is who is doing the analysis. In the board-confidence approach, it is the ERM team leading this task. In the management-value approach, it is the risk owner and his or her analysis team who perform the analysis by responding to each of the enterprise risks illustrated in the template.

In my experience, as we continued discussions with risk coordinators and risk sponsors, some of the risks evolved as we learned more about them. In particular, we found that some enterprise risks we had originally defined as one were actually two, and had to be redefined and described accordingly.

> The information in sections 2, 3, and 4 would enable an effective rating of the risk's impact and likelihood, most likely by the risk owner and sponsor. The companies I have worked with have elected not to do that because all enterprise risks were rated separately through a survey process. This decision would depend upon your complete approach to ERM; however, I believe it could be advantageous.

As I mentioned in chapter 1, ERM is never "done." These forms (and the forms described in step 4 below) need to be updated regularly, the timing of which depends on factors specific to the company, including the progress of ERM. My experience indicates that the updates tend to occur about every 18 months. During the updates, it is quite acceptable to limit the interviews to only the risk coordinator and/or risk sponsor, and not involve the supporting managers and supervisors.

When my team and I completed the inherent risk summary forms through interviews with management, we found it helpful to create some supporting documentation, mostly for ourselves. Behind each of the numbered items on the form, we wrote an explanatory paragraph or two to ensure we had a clear understanding of what certain terms meant or what selected activities entailed. This is information we gathered during the interviews by asking the right questions. You could share this internal documentation with the risk coordinators, but doing so is likely to lead to a lot of back-and-forth wordsmithing that may be overkill for this particular documentation. I suggest keeping it in the ERM team as supporting notes to refer to as needed.

Step 4. Roll inherent risk information up to the enterprise risk.

Once you have completed the inherent risk summary forms, there is one more step to the enterprise risk analysis. There is a second, different, form (see **exhibit 5.4**), and it is different for a reason.

The executive summary form is what the senior executives and board members will most likely prefer to read. They can be provided the inherent risk summary forms as supporting documentation for their review if they wish, but many will focus primarily on the executive summary. If you have 19 enterprise risks in your risk inventory, you will complete and provide to the board 19 executive summary forms. I recommend providing the information to your executives and board as a professional-looking book with the executive summary forms preceding each set of supporting inherent risk summaries.

Exhibit 5.4: Example Executive Summary: Environmental, Health, and Safety	
Risk Category	
Environmental, Health, and Safety—The risk of conducting business in a manner that results in employee harm or environmental damage	
Risk Sponsor: John Smith, EVP, Operations	**Risk Coordinator:** Jane Doe, VP, EHS
Inherent Risks	
1. **Health and safety**—Potential failure to perform tasks safely and maintain the health of employees 2. **EHS compliance**—Potential failure to comply with environmental laws and regulations resulting in environmental damage, fines, or sanctions	
Strengths	
1. **Company's EHS policy**—The company's EHS policy demonstrates the company's commitment to safety and the environment. 2. **Monthly safety leadership meetings**—The company safety leadership team, consisting of executives at the highest levels, meets monthly to determine ways of improving the company's safety performance, systems, and culture. 3. **Serious accident process**—Corrective actions and lessons learned from actual accidents are investigated to identify root causes.	
Opportunities/Issues	
High-risk activities: It is the nature of the business for company employees to perform high-risk activities that could result in serious injuries and/or fatalities. The company has not recently evaluated the employees' safety performance.	

The executive summary is the rollup and expansion of the work done on the inherent risk summary forms. It contains:

- A definition of the enterprise risk—again, developed in consultation with the risk coordinator and risk sponsor—as well as the names of those two individuals. It lists each of the inherent risks within the enterprise risk, with their definition, taken straight from the inherent risk summary forms.

- A Strengths section, which is different from the inherent risk summary, and is something the ERM team develops with the risk sponsor and coordinator based on the information included in section 3 of the inherent risk summary forms. It focuses on the most important risk management activities already in place and defines each.

- An Opportunities/Issues section, which lists a selection of the most significant items that appear in section 4 of the inherent risk summary forms. Not all opportunities/issues listed in the inherent risk summary have to be rolled up to the enterprise risk.

Once you have completed the sheet, be sure to run it by the risk sponsor and get his or her approval that it is ready to be shared with the full executive team and board. This serves a couple of purposes. First and foremost, it is a courtesy to ensure the risk sponsor is comfortable with the content. Second, it makes it clear that the individual is not only the sponsor of the enterprise risk and its associated inherent risks but also of the supporting documentation and, therefore, any questions about those items should be directed to him or her.

A Summary of Steps and Outputs Described in This Chapter

Steps

1. Set up an interview with the risk coordinator for each enterprise risk to review the definition and gather the top two to four inherent risks in the enterprise risk.
2. Populate your one-page enterprise risk inventory with the enterprise risks and associated inherent risks.
3. For each of the inherent risks on the risk inventory, complete section 1 (risk sponsor and risk coordinator only), section 2, and section 3 of an inherent risk summary form.
4. Set up an interview with the risk coordinators (and their managers and supervisors as needed) to review sections 2 and 3 for their enterprise risk.
5. Use the information to flesh out sections 2 and 3 and draft the definition and scope in section 1.
6. Set up an interview with the risk coordinators to review the definition and scope for their enterprise risk and to gather information for sections 4 and 5.
7. Complete the inherent risk summary form for all enterprise risks.

8. Begin the executive summary form by setting up an appointment with the risk sponsors and coordinators to discuss the definition for their enterprise risk and the Strengths section.

9. Complete the executive summary form for each enterprise risk and get approval from the appropriate risk sponsor.

10. Provide the executive summary forms and the inherent risk forms to the company's executives and board of directors, according to the process used by your company.

Outputs

- A comprehensive, customized **enterprise risk inventory**, which lists on one page the enterprise risks and the inherent risks in each
- A completed **inherent risk summary** form for each inherent risk that defines the risk and its scope, names its sponsor and coordinator, and lists its contributing factors and risk management activities, any critical gaps, and risk management plans expected to have a positive impact on the risk over time
- A completed **executive summary** form for each enterprise risk that defines the risk, names its sponsor and coordinator, lists and defines its inherent risks, identifies strengths already existing to mitigate the risks, and identifies and defines critical issues

CHAPTER 6

BOARD-CONFIDENCE APPROACH: ENTERPRISE RISK ASSESSMENT

This chapter describes how to build and deploy an annual risk survey, summarize the results, and use a variety of charts to report the results in a meaningful way.

At this point in the board-confidence approach, you have successfully developed a customized comprehensive inventory of enterprise risks and key inherent risks that reside in each. You have worked closely with management to define and gain a much better understanding of each of the inherent risks and, in the aggregate, each enterprise risk. Through the enterprise risk analysis effort so far, using simple terms, you have a:

Enterprise Risk Analysis	Enterprise Risk Workshops
Enterprise Risk Assessment	Enterprise Risk Reporting

1. Thorough understanding of the things that could go wrong (risks).

2. Good idea about key factors that do, or can, contribute to things going wrong (contributing factors).

3. Much better understanding of activities in place to help keep things from going wrong (risk management activities).

4. Clear view of any gaps between contributing factors and risk management activities that, if ignored, could allow a significant risk to occur (opportunities for improvement).

5. Solid grasp on action plans that are expected to manage significant contributing factors and help keep things from going wrong in the future (risk management plans).

Some might think an assessment of enterprise risk is done after you complete your initial six to nine months of hard work creating the enterprise risk inventory and analysis. Not so fast. What we must remember is that most of the information obtained during the enterprise risk analysis effort was done through a facilitation of a SME's self-assessment of risks in his or her areas of responsibility. That means two things could be inherently built in your information. The SME could be 1) trying to present a more positive picture of the risk area for which he or she is primarily responsible for managing, or 2) presenting a worse picture than reality to get his or her preferred special project funded as the risk gets more attention from management. Through two decades of listening to SMEs, my guess is that more than 90 percent told the story exactly as they saw it, but we should be alert to potential bias and blind spots.

Once you have the right enterprise risk inventory and analysis customized for your company, it is time to complete an enterprise risk assessment. The enterprise risk assessment will help you to determine the residual risks from a broader stakeholder perspective. These are the risks, if any, that are of concern after considering the related contributing factors and risk management activities. Since ERM has been around for many years, there are a good number of proven approaches out there that can help you determine the residual risks of most concern. Because it is one of the most efficient approaches, I recommend you consider using an online risk survey to assess the enterprise risks across the organization. Although I am not the biggest fan of surveys, especially to gain insight on very complex enterprise risks, I am going to share with you a survey approach to assessing risks that has impressed me and proved to be very impactful for a *Fortune* 250 company, now for more than eight years. The key to the survey success is to directly leverage the customized enterprise risk inventory.

> This chapter's title uses the phrase *enterprise risk assessment,* which is a term that may mean different things among ERM professionals, risk specialists, and internal auditors across the world. In the ERM context, an enterprise risk assessment identifies the risks that matter most to the executive team and the board. It is not intended to address risk in a way that primarily enables a corporate risk manager to identify key "insurable" risks or an internal auditor to develop a traditional audit plan. Instead, it focuses on the risks to the execution of the enterprise's strategy and achievement of its objectives. It helps management and the board understand the view from the top: what the company's leaders consider the most significant risks to the organization.

The Annual Enterprise Risk Survey

The first thing to say about doing a survey is that if you do not design it correctly and get enough serious leadership participation, you may end up wasting time. A company I worked with achieved 100 percent participation in the enterprise risk survey year after year. Why? Because the people surveyed (about 75 of the top leaders and executives of the business) knew how important it was to provide their point of view.

They also knew that the results of the survey, including the response rate, would be shared with the leadership, executive management, and the board. In fact, it was common for the CEO to ask if we had 100 percent participation. If not, he sometimes would ask who did not complete the survey. We were cautious about providing the CEO any name(s), but for those one or two stragglers, we did remind them that we may be asked which leaders did not think the risk assessment for the executive and board was worth a little of their time.

Although we usually got 100 percent participation, that does not mean that everyone completed the survey by the original deadline. In fact, we found that about 75 to 80 percent responded without prompting, while the remaining one-quarter needed a bit of encouragement. It was common for the ERM team to send out reminders and even make some calls to bring the final few across the finish line. I suggest you be prepared to do that follow-up and build in a little extra time in your project timeline. The value of the survey depends on it.

A couple of other words about the survey before we discuss its content and format:

- **Limit the length**. The people being surveyed are very busy. They understand the importance of ERM and want to contribute to its success, but their time (and patience) is limited. The survey described below limits the time needed for completion by its very structure.

- **Give them the right amount of time to get the survey completed**. The leaders have a lengthy to-do list every day, so it would be unreasonable to ask them to complete the survey within a few days. They need to schedule some quiet time in their agendas. On the other hand, if you give them too much time, it may get lost in the shuffle or you will lose the momentum you built up during the analysis process. In my experience, two or three weeks is about right.

Building the Survey

By completing the analysis first, you have already made a huge start on the survey itself. The basic premise of the survey is to focus on the enterprise risks from the enterprise risk inventory (remember, there are typically 15 to 20 enterprise risks), and for each, ask the respondents to provide their view on four aspects: the impact, the likelihood, the velocity with which it might occur, and the enterprise's preparedness for it. So, if there are 19 enterprise risks, each survey participant will have to provide 76 responses. Yes, the number of clicks adds up quickly, even if you are surveying only 19 risks. This is a good reason, among others, to avoid surveying all of the 55 to 60 inherent risks.

Eighty responses may seem like a lot, especially since I have just suggested you keep the survey short. The solution to that conundrum is to fashion the survey in such a way that each response requires a single click of the mouse. The following description is how my ERM teams formatted the online survey. It took several years of experimentation to develop this approach to ensure quality results and full participation. It is certainly not the only way it could be done, but I am comfortable recommending it because I know it works. We estimate the survey takes about 30 to 45 minutes to complete. Also, remember, if you want to use only two rating criteria (i.e., impact and likelihood), the participants would need to provide only 40 responses, using about half the time.

This is a good time to remind ourselves that the participants are actually rating an enterprise risk versus a category of risks. The enterprise risk is simply a more broadly defined potential risk event that could happen, within which the supporting inherent risks fall. Here are some examples of enterprise risk:

Procurement—The risk of relying too heavily on a single source supplier.

EHS—The risk of conducting business in a manner that results in employee harm or environmental damage.

Disasters—The risk of ineffective planning for a major disaster, causing business interruption.

The first screen of the online survey includes a brief statement of the purpose of the survey and the handling of the results, assurance of the confidentiality of the responses, and a thank you for participating. This should be one brief paragraph. My team generally issued the survey to separate groups so we could easily accumulate the results by the level or department the leader represented. Some survey tools allow more options for identifying survey participant demographics.

After the brief introduction, the survey begins. The next screen (see **exhibit 6.1**) describes the four criteria to be evaluated during the survey: financial impact, likelihood, preparedness, and velocity. The responses illustrated in **exhibit 6.1** are sample responses that could be used depending upon the size of the organization, its financial/business objectives, or risk tolerance. For example, the financial impact ranges below may be most appropriate for a company with $10 to $15 billion in annual revenue.

Exhibit 6.1: Survey Screen Introducing the Survey Criteria
Enterprise Risk Management Survey
Risk Assessment
This survey uses your expertise to help us gain perspective around potential risk impact, likelihood, preparedness, and velocity. Please rate as many risks as possible. Your rating should consider the potential impact to the company as a whole and not necessarily how it would impact your specific area. However, if you do not have a point of view on a risk, feel free to leave it blank. If a potential risk is not included, please add it in the box provided on the last page of the survey.

First, rate the potential financial impact of each risk, from 1 to 5. 1. <$50 million 2. >$50 million and <$250 million 3. >$250 million and <$500 million 4. >$500 million and <$1 billion 5. >$1 billion	**Second,** rate the likelihood of this risk occurring. 1. Very unlikely 2. Unlikely 3. Somewhat likely 4. Likely 5. Very likely
Third, rate how prepared the company is for this particular risk. 1. Very prepared 2. Prepared 3. Somewhat prepared 4. Unprepared 5. Very unprepared	**Fourth,** rate the velocity of how quickly the company would be impacted after the occurrence of the risk event. 1. Greater than one year 2. One year 3. Weeks to months 4. Days to weeks 5. Hours to days
Please enter your name (optional):	

The next screen (see **exhibit 6.2**) lists some enterprise risks (from **exhibit 4.2**) with their definitions (from the executive summary discussed in chapter 5). My team often put on a single screen about four enterprise risks representing a major section of risks (e.g.,

Strategic on slide 1, Operations on slide 2). We wanted the participants to be thinking about related risks as each screen was completed.

The response boxes appear next to the enterprise risk and its definition. The first one asks the respondent to estimate the financial impact to the organization if the inherent risks in that specific enterprise risk materialize. When the participant clicks on the title "Financial Impact," the list of dropdown response options outlined in **exhibit 6.1** appears and the respondent selects one).

Exhibit 6.2: Example Screen of Survey Questions				
Enterprise Risk Management Survey				
Operations Risk Category				
Procurement—The risk of relying too heavily on a single source provider.				
EHS—The risk of conducting business in a manner that results in employee harm or environmental damage.				
Disasters—The risk of ineffective planning for a major disaster, causing business interruption.				
Operational Risks—Ratings				
	Financial Impact	Likelihood	Preparedness	Velocity
Procurement	⌄	⌄	⌄	⌄
EHS	⌄	⌄	⌄	⌄
Disasters	⌄	⌄	⌄	⌄

> This survey demonstrates why it is so important to use a common language that everyone understands and agrees on when developing the risk analysis. Without that, the survey participants' responses may not be as meaningful because they are not operating from a shared, consistent understanding of the enterprise risk.

I would like to pause a moment and offer a little advice. As risk specialists, we sometimes overcomplicate things and bring in all the risk jargon we can find. Over the last two decades, I have observed and sometimes been involved in debates over risk rating criteria. Should we use a rating scale of 1 to 3, 1 to 5, or 1 to 7? Should we use two criteria, four criteria, or even more? Should we keep it very simple—high, medium, low? Should we make it more scientific—$XXX impact, degree of reputational damage, seriousness of injury/death?

My feeling is that it does not really make that much difference. I have used most of the above, and more. In most situations, it comes down to the fact that at this stage, these are all opinion-based responses. With that said, I do realize that executives in some industries (e.g., financial services) may make better decisions based upon hard numbers, statistics, or models, whereas other executives (e.g., oil and gas) tend to make decisions based upon less scientific numbers. I have heard many times, "We don't need to know if it could impact our company $1,232,554,000 if the risk occurs." Just having a reasonable, solid estimated potential impact of about $1 billion is enough to further analyze the enterprise risk and take action as needed.

Summarizing and Communicating the Results

The first step is to aggregate the responses from all participants for each question. This will help indicate how to prioritize the enterprise risks (see **exhibit 6.3**). There are different ways to prioritize the enterprise risks based on the responses. Some enterprises may use a weighting system, but my ERM teams have usually taken the more direct route, simply adding together the top responses to create a single priority score for each enterprise risk. With this option, understand that risk number 1 may not be that different from risk number 2 or 3; however, the top few risks are more likely to be of more concern than the bottom four or five. Lastly, all of the risks are critical to the business, no matter what the ranking.

Board-Confidence Approach: Enterprise Risk Assessment

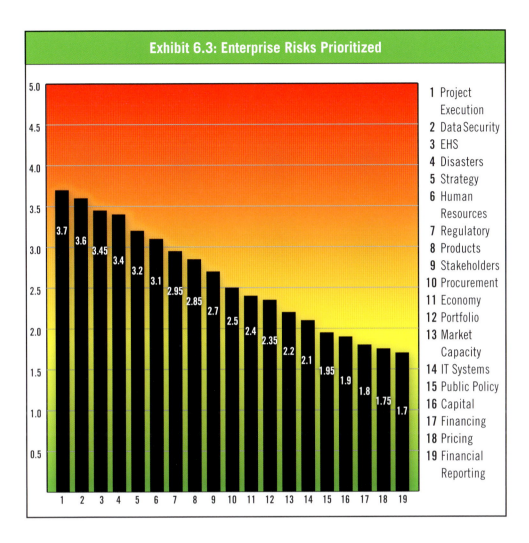

It may also be interesting and useful to compare the results from different types of respondents (see **exhibit 6.4**). For example, do the priority rankings reported year to year, or by the executive team and the VPs, or the executive team and the subject matter experts generally align? Distinct, marked differences, as indicated by the circle in the graph, may indicate something as simple as a different level of understanding of the risk or a different perspective, or they may reveal a troubling need for greater communication and deeper discussion across the enterprise.

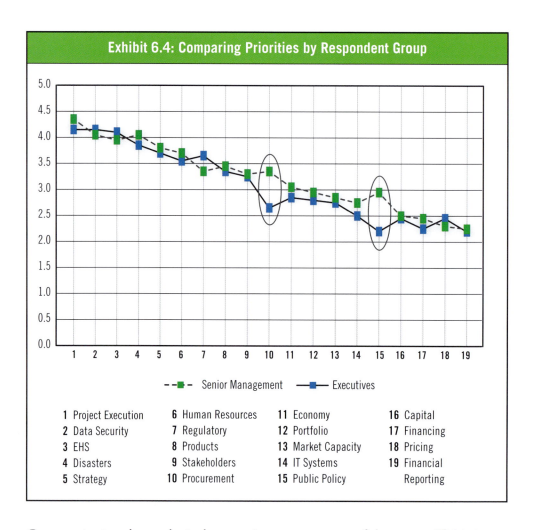

Communicating the results is the most important aspect of the survey. If this is not done in an understandable, meaningful, and actionable way, much of the effort of conducting the survey could be in vain. Finding visual representations of the data that enable quick and easily discernible conclusions is the key. Two such charts have already been shown (see **exhibits 6.3** and **6.4**). The heat map (bubble chart) has also been well received because it enables a better view into each of the four areas covered on the survey: financial impact, likelihood, velocity, and preparedness (see **exhibit 6.5**). And, remember, management is very familiar with these charts as we have been using them year after year.

Board-Confidence Approach: Enterprise Risk Assessment

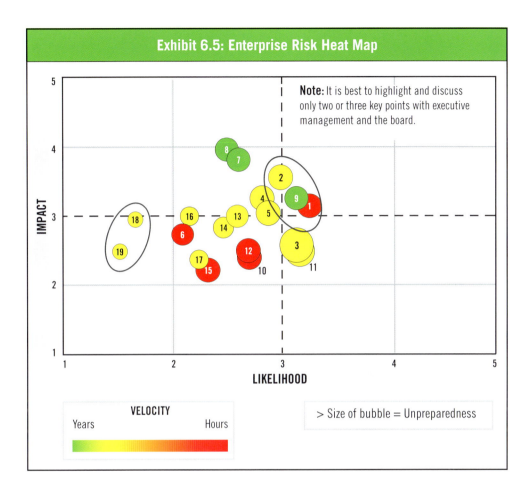

Again, I would like to offer a little advice. Some organizations have become stuck on assessing risk and developing heat maps, calling that "ERM." In response, some more experienced ERM specialists are saying that heat maps are of no value. I, on the other hand, will stand by most all heat maps used by my clients and organizations because they proved to be very effective tools for communicating significant risks. The heat map illustrated in **exhibit 6.5**, in particular, allowed executive management to engage in healthy, meaningful discussions about risks that matter most to shareholders and other stakeholders.

Much of the success of the heat map is far more about the "what" and "how" of the presentation of it rather than the map itself. Less effective heat maps tend to fall short for any number of reasons, most common being user error. Examples of the ways presentations of heat maps may fail include:

- The heat map's presenters may get bogged down in the detail (showing 50-plus risks on the map) or use risk statements that make little sense to management.

- They may try to self-rate the risks or overemphasize the heat map's exactness.

- They may present the heat map as a true, quantified version of risks, when in reality it is probably based on opinions, not scientifically proven modeling techniques.

- They do not understand exactly what every bubble on the chart means and how it relates to the others.

- They do not stick to the common language used in the analysis. Switching back to jargon at this point will result in losing the audience, particularly management; and if management does not understand the discussion, it is not the tool's failure, it is the presenters'.

As you may notice in the heat map in **exhibit 6.5**, the information is presented cleanly and in a meaningful way. Each of the four criteria is clearly labeled and identified on the chart. One chief audit executive (CAE) used to say, somewhat in jest, "We don't want any big red bubbles in the upper right quadrant." Based on the four rating criteria, a big red bubble in the upper right quadrant means you have a risk that is likely to occur, will be fast-developing, and pack a powerful financial punch for which the organization is unprepared.

I have seen a discussion of the heat map work very effectively in helping management agree that a significant risk needed more attention. As a result of the discussion, attention was given to the risk, and when the risk later materialized, the company survived the impact. I do not claim that the company felt no impact, but I do know that the same risk significantly crippled other companies in the industry because they were not as prepared.

Even though heat maps can be effective, I now tend to use all types of vehicles to communicate risks to executives and the board. As for the survey, I know that approach to assessing risk and the resulting discussion work quite well.

Of course, even the most definitive survey results can fall short unless they are shared with the appropriate audiences. My ERM team discussed the results, especially emerging risks and issues, with the executive team and reported the risks to the audit committee and the board of directors. In fact, executives, audit committee members, and other board members expected to see the survey results year after year. The appropriate groups may differ in other enterprises depending on the organization's structure, policies, processes, and culture.

> The point is to elevate the right risks, to the right people, at the right time.

A Summary of Steps and Outputs Described in This Chapter

Steps

1. Create an effective online enterprise risk survey.
2. Issue the request to leaders to complete the survey and follow up as needed to gain 100 percent participation.
3. Prepare the charts reflecting the results, e.g., prioritization of enterprise risks, comparison of responses of different groups, heat map.
4. Distribute the results to the appropriate individuals/groups.

Outputs

- A survey that gathers opinions on the financial impact, likelihood, velocity, and preparedness of the enterprise risks reflected in the risk inventory
- Charts and reports reflecting the results of the survey

CHAPTER 7

BOARD-CONFIDENCE APPROACH: ENTERPRISE RISK WORKSHOPS

This chapter describes how to prepare for and conduct a series of risk workshops, report the results of the workshops, and seek feedback on the workshops to enable continuous improvement.

This chapter provides insight on another major component of the board-confidence approach to ERM—enterprise risk workshops (risk workshops). The primary purpose of the risk workshops is to allow a cross-functional team of SVPs, VPs, and select managers to openly discuss risks within three or four related enterprise risks during a two-hour working session.

Enterprise Risk Analysis	Enterprise Risk Workshops
Enterprise Risk Assessment	Enterprise Risk Reporting

The risk workshops are conducted year-round. Although the same enterprise risks included in the survey are considered during the workshops, the timing of the risk workshops is not directly related to the timing of the enterprise risk survey. In fact, no survey results are considered during the risk workshops. Conversely, the risk workshops do have some direct relationship with the enterprise risk analysis and tend to come after the analysis is completed/updated.

Back to the Enterprise Risk Inventory

The enterprise risk inventory developed in chapters 4 and 5 proves its worth yet again as an integral part of the risk workshops. Before you schedule your first risk workshop, take a look at your enterprise risk inventory and package three or four related risks together. Your broad sections of risks—Strategic, Operations, Corporate, and Financial—can be used as a starting point. Within the Operations section, a sample package of related enterprise risks could include Environmental, Health, and Safety (EHS), Disasters, and Portfolio (see **exhibit 7.1**).

Some expected participants would include leaders such as the VP of IT, VP of EHS, director of disaster recovery, senior security director, and the VP of portfolio management. You may also include some EHS managers to hear a little deeper perspective on specific EHS areas such as environmental, employee safety, and EHS compliance. It is common to have 10 to 15 participants in a risk workshop. The goal is to limit the group to the top leaders for the selected enterprise risks and provide an open and honest dialog. Too many people and too many different job levels can inhibit free and frank discussion, depending upon the culture at your company.

> If your enterprise risk inventory has an enterprise risk that stands alone and does not relate to any of the others, it is fine to hold a workshop for only that risk with related cross-functional leaders.

The risk workshops have proven to be a very effective way of finding out which risks merit more attention from the executive team. The discussion also helps identify any significant emerging risks that may not be on management's radar quite yet and changes in known risks already documented in the enterprise risk inventory. One of the major benefits of directly involving leaders in these cross-functional risk workshops, as well as ERM overall, is that the executive team trusts these leaders (SMEs) on a daily basis to help the company be successful.

It is important to invite the right SMEs to the right risk workshops. In fact, my team confirms the risk workshop participants with the executive team to make sure we do not miss anyone of significance. When we summarize and communicate risk workshop results with the executive team, they have a tendency to believe and seriously consider the results because they know where the information came from: their selected SMEs.

Exhibit 7.1: Grouping of Enterprise Risk for the Inventory

STRATEGIC

Stakeholders	Strategy	Public Policy	Economy
• Core Customers • Investors • Community	• Strategy Development • Strategy Execution • Competition	• Public Policy • Political Climate	• National Economic Conditions • Global Economic Conditions

OPERATIONS

Procurement	Project Execution	Products	Market Capacity
• Suppliers • Materials Management • Logistics	• Project Prioritization • Project Management	• Core Products • Product Management • Product Costs	• Capacity • Facilities

Data Security	Portfolio	Environmental, Health, and Safety	Disasters
• Data Governance • Data Quality • Data Classification	• Portfolio Strategy • Investment Decisions	• Health and Safety • Environmental Stewardship • EHS Compliance	• Natural Hazards • Terrorism • Explosion/Fire

CORPORATE

Human Resources	IT Systems	Regulatory
• Recruitment • Retention • Employee Development • Work Environment	• IT Governance • Business Continuity • Information Security	• Regulation Awareness • Regulatory Compliance

FINANCIAL

Capital	Pricing	Financing	Financial Reporting
• Capital Availability • Investment	• Price Strategy • Price Volatility	• Counterparty Credit • Credit Rate	• Information Accuracy • Financial Reporting

> This is a good time to share my experience regarding management's perceptions of information received for consideration. Earlier in my career, I was part of a more traditional internal audit team that was reviewing risks and controls at a refinery operation. Among other items of concern, we reported some very meaningful insights regarding potential efficiency gains to the refinery's operations. These results were primarily obtained through one-on-one interviews with the SMEs at the refinery who did not hold back on expressing their concerns because we had quickly gained their trust. After the audit was complete, we shared the results with the president, who appeared to appreciate the information.
>
> About a year or so later, we visited with the new president of the petroleum subsidiary and, during our discussion, he referred to the last refinery audit report and said he believed it had some very good information about the refinery operations. I asked if much action had been taken on the results and, somewhat surprisingly, he said, "Not much." He explained that management simply chose not to fully act upon the results because the information came from audit. (By the way, our audit department was generally well respected across the management team.) It did not seem to matter that we actually obtained the information from the operations management. That was when I discovered that for any process that involves gaining insight into the risks or issues facing the company, management is much more likely to believe and seriously consider information it knows came from trusted employees. I experienced this over and over, company to company, for many years. Therefore, it would be wise to emphasize insights gained through collaboration with SMEs and employees.

It takes about 12 months to conduct enough risk workshops to cover the 19 enterprise risks and related inherent risks. My team usually waited a month or so after completing the enterprise risk analysis to start the first risk workshop. Different schedules may work for different organizations based upon their cultures and level of ERM maturity.

Before we get into the specific steps taken to run an effective risk workshop, I want to share a few important points. First, and most important, the risk workshop is not just another meeting. Many meetings are not very productive or a good use of management's time. To be most effective, the ERM team needs to adequately plan and prepare for the workshop. At a high level, this includes setting a clear agenda, reviewing related enterprise risk analysis, developing materials necessary to support voting, preparing presentation slides, and customizing voting questions.

> The board-confidence approach to ERM is intended to minimize management's time commitment to ERM; therefore, it is intentionally less intrusive to management and far more reliant on the ERM team to facilitate most activities. Management, however, still remains responsible for the risk information and its accuracy.

Facilitating an Effective Risk Workshop

At the risk workshop, provide the participants with the materials they need to engage in the discussion. We found over time that the ideal background material consists of the executive summary for each enterprise risk being addressed in the workshop (as you developed in the enterprise risk analysis, discussed in chapter 5), followed by the inherent risk summary pages for the inherent risks in those enterprise risks (also chapter 5). If you are covering three enterprise risks in a workshop, you can expect to include 12 to 15 inherent risks, meaning the handout would be 15 to 18 pages. Again, the intent is to keep things simple and manageable.

This material gives the participants a refresher, if they need it, as to how the enterprise risk and supporting inherent risks have been defined and characterized. It ensures—again—a common language for the discussion. But, remember, while you are providing the executive summary of the selected enterprise risks as background information, most likely you will not be discussing them in detail during this workshop.

To focus everyone on the inherent risks (technically they are now residual risks), my team found it useful to provide one additional handout consisting of two sets of information. One is a listing of the inherent risks to be discussed in the workshop, the two questions that will be asked about each, and a blank table with columns labeled "Actual," "Desired," and "Gap" (see **exhibit 7.2**). The other information on the handout is a description of the values of the response scale (see **exhibit 7.3**).

Exhibit 7.2: Example Inherent Risk Handout for the Workshop			
Risk Category/Inherent Risks	**Actual**	**Desired**	**Gap**
Portfolio			
• Portfolio Strategy			
• Investment Decisions			
Environmental, Health, and Safety			
• Health and Safety			
• Environmental Stewardship			
• EHS Compliance			
Disasters			
• Natural Hazards			
• Terrorism			
• Explosion/Fire			

This keeps everyone focused on the workshop's scope (inherent risks), what will be voted on (two questions), and what their responses mean. It also gives those who like to keep track of their own voting a place to capture that information.

> Effective facilitation takes training and experience. Some relevant course topics I recommend include executive presentation skills, interpersonal skills, facilitation skills, managing conflict, voting technology training, and identifying personality styles. Most important is improving the skills you learn by actually facilitating workshops.

\multicolumn{2}{c}{**Exhibit 7.3: Rating Scale for Workshop Questions**}
\multicolumn{2}{c}{1. How effectively are we managing this risk? (Actual) 2. How effectively should we be managing this risk? (Desired)}
Scale	**Rating Definitions**
1 Minimally Effective	**Minimally Effective** • Few of the risk management activities in place are effectively performed and make an adequate contribution to mitigating the risk. • For the most part, opportunities/issues or contributing factors are not managed well, resulting in a high likelihood of a risk occurring with a significant impact to the company. • Risk management plans need to be developed and implemented to effectively manage the risk.
2 ...	
3 Moderately Effective	**Moderately Effective** • Some risk management activities are in place and are performed well enough to help mitigate the risk. • Meaningful opportunities/issues or contributing factors are not managed well, resulting in a medium likelihood of a risk occurring with a significant impact to the company. • Some risk management plans need to be developed and implemented to effectively manage the risk.
4 ...	
5 Effective	**Effective** • Well-designed risk management activities are in place and are performed adequately, resulting in effective management of the risk. • Few to no opportunities/issues or contributing factors exist, resulting in a low likelihood of a risk occurring with a significant impact to the company. • Few, if any, risk management plans need to be developed and implemented to effectively manage the risk.
6 ...	
7 Very Effective	**Very Effective** • All needed risk management activities are in place and are performed well, resulting in very effective management of the risk. • No opportunities/issues or contributing factors exist, resulting in a remote likelihood of a risk occurring with a significant impact to the company. • No risk management plans need to be developed and implemented to effectively manage the risk.

Voting on Inherent Risks

To quickly focus our discussion on the most important inherent risks, my team would facilitate the participants through a quick voting process during the first 15 minutes of the two-hour workshop. Supporting workshops with effective voting technology has contributed to interesting and effective discussions for decades. Voting technology—when it is used correctly—has proven to be effective for risk workshops. Most participants enjoy casting their confidential vote and having it immediately displayed along with other participants' votes in easy-to-read bar charts. The key is to use the technology strategically and sparingly during the workshop. Whatever voting technology you use, make it very simple and operator-friendly. If you are going to implement quality ERM, it is worth investing in software and hardware that is dedicated to capturing, tallying, and displaying votes effectively and efficiently.

Now, on to the voting. You can address the inherent risks in any order. Let's say, from our example, we focus first on Health and Safety, an inherent risk in the EHS enterprise risk. For that and all the other inherent risks, we ask two questions:

1. How well are we managing this risk? With regard to the responses, my team used a 7-point scale ranging from 1 (Minimally Effective) to 7 (Very Effective) as shown in **exhibit 7.3**. Other organizations may use a 5-point scale, a 9-point scale, or any number of other scales. The number of values on the scale is not important as long as the scale is not cumbersome or confusing for the respondents to use and it provides results that are reasonable and meaningful to you.

2. How well should we be managing this risk? In other words, how important is it to effectively manage the risk?

A good voting system will automatically tally the average response for each question and display the results via bar charts, revealing the gap between the two (see **exhibit 7.4**). So, if the average rating for how well we manage Health and Safety is 3.5 and the average rating for how well we should manage it is 6.7, we have a gap—or opportunity for improvement—of 3.2. It is in the gap where issues (contributing factors) and opportunities tend to reside.

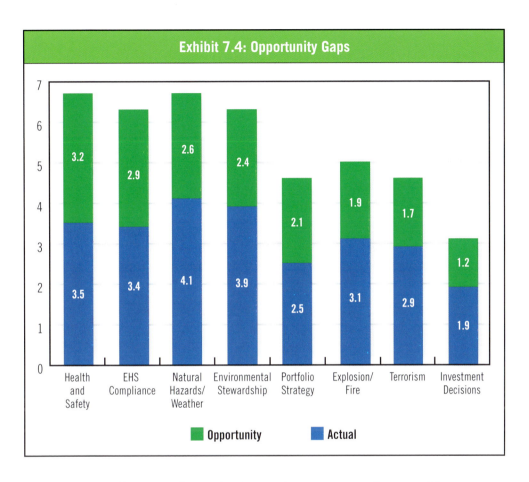

As you may recall, we voted on risks during the enterprise risk survey. There are two reasons this voting exercise differs from the survey, and those reasons lead to a deeper level of understanding:

- The annual enterprise risk survey asks many non-SMEs (along with a few SMEs) to vote on areas they may not know much about. For the survey, the leaders are asked to provide their best estimate of financial impact, likelihood, velocity, and preparedness about enterprise risks with which they may have limited familiarity. At one of my past companies, we encouraged all survey participants to think like the CEO, who has to care and know about the entire company, significant risks across the enterprise, and all of its stakeholder needs. Because these are business leaders, they tend to do a good job of that; however, they are often voting about an area that is not in their primary area of responsibility. In the risk workshops, we are talking only to the SMEs for a select few enterprise risks. Assuming you have successfully created an open and honest environment, their opinions tend to better reflect "the truth" about the current status of the risk.

- The survey focuses on the 19 or so enterprise risks. In the workshop, we go one step deeper to the inherent risks listed in the enterprise risks.

Discussing and Communicating the Results

After quickly completing the voting process, we facilitate an open, knowledgeable discussion among a cross-functional group of respected leaders. Typically, the discussion begins on the areas with the largest opportunity gaps. As facilitators for the workshop, my team would ask questions like: Why is there a gap? What is driving the concern about this risk? What are we doing to manage it? The discussion for one risk could last 10 minutes or it could last 30 minutes. The key is to move on once points start being repeated and it seems clear that there is no further room to explore the topic.

> Sometimes as risk specialists or internal auditors, we tend to want to ensure full coverage of all topics on the agenda (i.e., inherent risks). This usually results in a "check the box" exercise and/or documenting a lot of broad, high-level information about all the risks, which does not provide enough insight to truly take action. During a risk workshop, we can take all the time we need on any one risk. That is why we start with the risk of most concern, knowing we are not likely to get through all the risks voted on. It is okay to discuss only three of 15 inherent risks, as long as they are the three right risks.

That does not mean you avoid discussing the lower-gap items. After you cover the larger-gap risks, ask if there is anything in the remaining risks anyone wants to talk about. Chances are those lower-gap items are the ones people feel comfortable about— they understand the risk and they know the measures that are being taken to address it. No need to discuss in this setting at this time.

Also, remember, because you have grouped related enterprise risks to be discussed in the workshop, chances are the inherent risks are interrelated as well. Discussing an inherent risk in one enterprise risk is likely to touch on an inherent risk in another, so one discussion may serve multiple purposes.

> Do not spend time in the workshop trying to "solve" a risk. There is not enough time to do that effectively, and probably not the right information available to make good decisions. Developing action plans, monitoring, and following up come later.

The resulting report from each workshop consists of the actual/opportunity charts for each inherent risk and some text where needed. You may want to group all those charts that are unremarkable (minimal gap, no discussion) together on one page and dedicate a second page to the ones that were significant and discussed in some detail. For those, in addition to providing the chart, add a brief recap of the discussion about the causes for the gap and current mitigation activities.

In one company where I worked, the summary of results was not considered "official" and, therefore, not distributed widely. We generally provided the summary to the workshop participants and the risk sponsors at the EVP level. At times, we shared some of the results with the executive team via the ERM steering committee and/or during monthly one-on-one meetings we had with the CEO.

After the reporting, that workshop is done. For the next workshop, start over again with two or three new grouped enterprise risks and facilitate another workshop with new people. The ERM team repeated this activity until all the enterprise risks were covered.

Sometimes people express concern that something might change in the 12 months since a particular inherent risk was last discussed, but it is useful to remind them that these workshops are not the only risk-related activity taking place in the organization. There are risk management activities and dedicated people working on risk every day of the year. If something significant changes, it will be noticed through one of the existing mitigating activities and can be addressed timely. Remember, most successful companies already have 85 to 90 percent of the necessary risk management processes and activities in place before you start ERM.

The key takeaway from the workshops is that the prioritization of the inherent risk (i.e., via voting) is not the purpose. The voting exists just to get the group started down the right track so meaningful discussions can be held. Do not waste time quibbling about statistics, models, and scales; start talking about what really matters: significant known or emerging risks that can have a significant impact on the company and its achievement of objectives.

Because my team was committed to a continuous improvement approach, we would conduct a survey (see **exhibit 7.5**) at the end of each workshop to help us gauge how well the workshop was received and how well it accomplished its purposes.

In keeping with the theme of this book—getting to the truth—it is nice to see that one of the consistently highest-rated questions was the first one: being able to speak openly and honestly in the workshop (see **exhibit 7.6**).

Exhibit 7.5: Post-Workshop Survey								
Workshop Survey: Your feedback is important to help us continually improve ERM. Please circle the rating that best reflects your opinion for each of the following statements. Also, any written comments will be appreciated.								
	Strongly Disagree	⋮	Disagree	⋮	Agree	⋮	Strongly Agree	
1. I was able to speak openly and honestly during the workshop.	1	2	3	4	5	6	7	
Comments:								
2. The workshop was productive.	1	2	3	4	5	6	7	
Comments:								
3. The right people were in the room to discuss the material.	1	2	3	4	5	6	7	
Comments:								
4. The workshop was long enough to cover the material.	1	2	3	4	5	6	7	
Comments:								
5. The voting technology enabled the workshop discussion.	1	2	3	4	5	6	7	
Comments:								
6. The voting technology could be used to enable other meetings.	1	2	3	4	5	6	7	
Comments:								
7. I am willing to participate in another risk workshop.	1	2	3	4	5	6	7	
Comments:								

Practical Enterprise Risk Management: Getting to the Truth

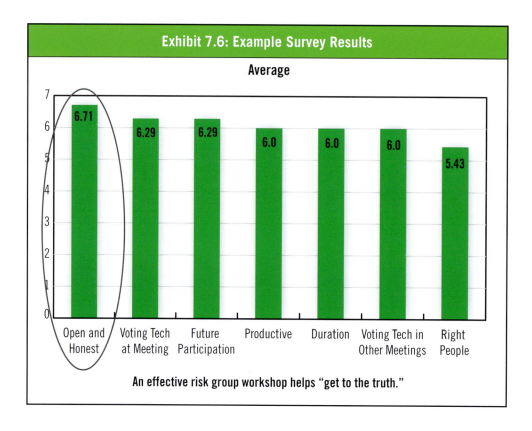

A Summary of Steps and Outputs Described in This Chapter
Steps

1. Group two or three related enterprise risks from the enterprise risk inventory and invite the appropriate risk coordinators and other high-level managers (including internal audit, as appropriate) to a two-hour workshop to vote and discuss known and emerging risks.

2. Create the background material and handout for the workshop. Assemble, program, and test the voting technology.

3. Facilitate the workshop, ensuring healthy open discussion on the risks that matter most.

4. Create the resulting report and distribute it to the appropriate individuals/groups.

5. Conduct a post-workshop survey to test the performance of the workshop.

6. Repeat steps 1 through 4. Continue until all enterprise risks have been covered in a risk workshop.

Outputs

- Background material and a handout for the workshop
- A survey that asks for a rating of the effectiveness of the current management and desired management of the inherent risks, and the gap between those two ratings
- Charts and reports reflecting the results of the surveys and discussions
- A post-workshop survey to test how well the workshop met its objectives

CHAPTER 8

KEY RISK AND PERFORMANCE INDICATORS

This chapter introduces key performance indicators and key risk indicators, and discusses their purpose and how they can interact to enable better understanding of significant risk and performance.

There is a well-known saying, "What gets measured, gets done." I tend to agree with that statement. Key performance indicators (KPIs) have been around a long time, and key risk indicators (KRIs) have now been around for some time as well. However, I believe we continue to have a lot to learn about both means of monitoring our company's performance and risks, especially at the entity level. In this chapter, I will share a very exciting project I managed while in strategic planning at a *Fortune* 250 company. Our initial focus was on KPIs, with the goal of KRIs subsequently becoming an integrated part of the key risk and performance indicators management system.

Some ERM practitioners choose to focus on monitoring risk through KRIs. While I agree that KRIs are critical to the successful monitoring of risks and implementation of ERM, I would like to suggest that there is value to be gained by beginning with measuring performance through KPIs. After that foundation is established, adding in KRIs will help you develop a seamless key risk and performance indicator management system.

At the entity level, these are largely uncharted waters. Most companies understand the value of KPIs and KRIs. However, to my knowledge, few have implemented an integrated key risk and performance indicator system at the entity level that truly drives value. We can start changing that mindset in this chapter.

> Before we go any further down the key risk and performance indicator path, I want to acknowledge that despite the benefits of this approach, it is possible that if you are a risk specialist or an internal auditor and you propose creating a performance measurement system, you may not have an opportunity to do so. In that case, perhaps you can focus on risk and KRIs, and then show management that you can do the same for performance through KPIs.

Getting Started with Performance Measurement

When the ERM team helps management put in place a key risk and performance indicator management system for the entity, working at the very top of the company, the system will provide management with better information on which to make business and strategic decisions. After all, we all know that accomplishing objectives is what everyone in the business is trying to achieve, including executives, operations management, line management, strategic planning personnel, performance management professionals, risk specialists, and internal auditors.

To get started, a formal project charter is highly recommended to clearly define the business case, problem statement, project objective, project scope, required resources, and project timeline. The problem statement and objective are especially important because they guide the decisions made throughout the project. An example problem statement may be: the company does not consistently focus on the activities and metrics that truly drive stakeholder value. The corresponding objective may then be: implement an ongoing KPI management process that directs focus on the true value drivers of the business and enhances transparency, thereby increasing action and accountability.

> We can already make the connection to KRI by changing only a few words in the objective statement: implement an ongoing *KRI* management process that directs focus on the true *risks* of the business and enhances transparency, thereby increasing action and accountability.

KPIs and KRIs are connected, but because some management tends to be more interested in performance than risk, it makes sense to start there and fold in KRIs later. I realize this may vary by industry, but in my experience, KPIs are more urgent and relevant to most management. KPIs reflect performance in the market and how well the company is doing compared to how well it said it would do. KRIs are indicators of things that *could* go wrong but have not gone wrong yet. So, management might say, "KRIs are not as relevant to me because I want to focus on what *is* going wrong (poor performance) and fix it more than I want to focus on what *might* go wrong." This is not the viewpoint of everyone at the management level, of course, but in my experience, when I have worked on setting up a KPI system, management has wanted it done as quickly as possible and was free with the resources needed to make it happen. When I moved on to KRIs, management was interested but showed less interest in speeding up the project's completion.

Building KPIs

Before starting to create KPIs, it is important to understand the differences between performance measures, metrics, and KPIs. Like risk information, performance information also suffers from the lack of a common language. Performance measurement systems have their own jargon, which includes many terms that may not be understood in the same way throughout the company. And, like risk, it is difficult to prioritize performance metrics—that is, identify the metrics that drive the most meaningful value for the business—when those involved in the prioritization effort do not share the same views on the most important metrics to measure.

> A **performance measure** is an indicator used by management to measure, report, and improve performance.

A **metric** is any standard of measurement.

A **KPI** is a selected metric that provides visibility into the performance of the business and enables decision makers to take action. KPIs are tied to a target and are chosen to give an indication of performance toward achievement of goals and objectives. KPIs tell us how well the business is performing and are used as a driver for improvement.

It is important to focus on the *key* part of KPI. Companies sometimes develop hundreds or even thousands of KPIs. This is overwhelming to employees and unwieldy for management. The same can be said for the number of KRIs. A successful system limits its KPIs to those that are most critical to driving business value and shareholder return (for publicly traded companies). In one company I worked with, that number was six, initially. Over time, each business unit had its own six, which aligned with the company's six.

Once you have defined your KPIs and set up systems to gather the appropriate information, you need a way to communicate the results succinctly to the executive level of the company. In other words, you need an executive dashboard: an easy-to-read graphical presentation (e.g., red, yellow, green) of the manageable number of KPIs you have developed to focus management's attention on the true value drivers of the business and shareholder return. It can be on paper, but it is far more effective if it is an online user interface that allows management immediate access to near-real-time information. An effective system will also allow management to hover the cursor over certain points for further explanation or different views of the data, such as by day or week, or by business unit.

> When in doubt, remember that every KPI is a metric, but not every metric is a KPI.

Having an executive dashboard that allows management to track performance on a near-real-time basis is a great tool (see **exhibit 8.1**). And, as performance is tracked regularly and performance starts tapering off, management may find itself raising the question, "What else could go wrong?" With that question, we enter the realm of risk and KRIs.

Key Risk and Performance Indicators

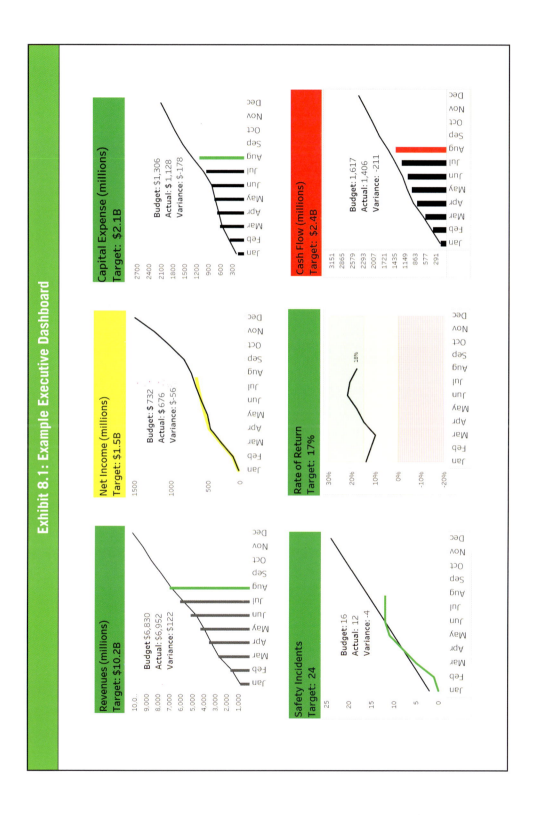

If you need any further confirmation of the close, symbiotic relationship between KPIs and KRIs, **exhibit 8.2** should provide it. It illustrates a KPI framework that was developed for a company I worked with. Note the striking similarity between the way it is presented and the language it uses, and the ERM framework depicted in **exhibit 2.1**.

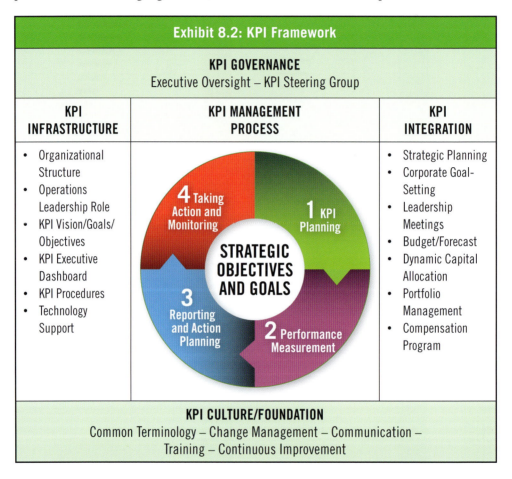

Adding in KRIs

Once the KPI management process is in place, you can follow a similar process to develop and integrate KRIs. Simply defined, a KRI is a selected metric that provides an early signal of increasing risk exposure. Coupling KRIs and KPIs can give management and the board significant insight into how effectively the organization manages risks and resolves performance issues.

Start by leveraging risk management's and internal audit's experience and ability, with both identifying emerging risks and helping management select the most critical KRIs. As noted previously, it is important to limit the selection to key indicators only, such as health and safety, operating cost, and capital and financing.

The KRIs can then be added to the KPI management system and viewed on an executive dashboard for real-time monitoring by executives, management, risk specialists, auditors, and other leaders. The ideal presentation is to combine the online KPI and KRI executive dashboards so that each perspective can be viewed by simply toggling back and forth.

Here is an example of the connection between KPIs and KRIs. Let's assume that your company has a goal relating to continuous improvement of EHS issues. An example of an EHS KPI might be the combined serious incident and fatality (SIF) rate, which measures the rate of recordable incidents that resulted in, or could have resulted in, a life-altering injury or fatality. The related enterprise risk might be the potential failure to perform tasks safely and maintain the health of employees, contractors, and the public. Therefore, the EHS KRI would entail measuring the number of incidents caused by mechanical design and integrity failure.

While the value of a KRI system seems clear, here is a word of warning. Developing KRIs can take a lot of time and resources. Of course, you can throw something together quickly, but if you want to create something that is meaningful and actionable, it can take quite a while and its success depends on a lot of decisions being made (e.g., what is the risk and what do we measure).

Ultimately, developing a combined key risk and performance indicator management system, as described in this chapter, can give management and the board significant insight into how effectively the company manages risks and resolves performance issues, both of which can impact the achievement of objectives. But this outcome will not come easily or quickly, and depends on the same types of critical success factors as ERM itself:

- Executive-level sponsorship
- Clear vision and scope (i.e., a project charter)

- A fully dedicated project champion (senior level)
- A project manager and detailed project plan
- Access to necessary SMEs and technical experts
- A focus on the few critical KPIs and KRIs
- Project structured into manageable pieces with key milestones
- A top-down approach
- A transition from project to process with dedicated people
- A project team that balances listening, learning, influencing, and driving

Generating business value depends on achieving or exceeding performance goals communicated to stakeholders. Retaining business value depends on understanding, monitoring, and managing significant risks to the achievement of strategic objectives. Having a core set of key indicators that reveal critical performance and risk can help management make effective decisions pertinent to the business's success. But, as I emphasized with ERM, just developing a system is not enough. With ERM, the true value comes when ERM is built into strategic planning, budgeting, forecasting, and other critical business functions. With KPIs and KRIs, the value exists in what you do with what you learn.

> In other words, measuring is not what is important; acting on the measures is.

CONCLUSION

No enterprise functions without risk. In fact, it is impossible to achieve any level of success without risk. However, too much risk, an unknown risk, or a known but underappreciated risk can be catastrophic for an organization, causing potentially unrecoverable financial, legal, or reputational damage.

In this book, I have tried to relate some of the practical experience I have gained during my two decades of pioneering and refining ERM within companies of all sizes and across all industries. I have chosen to describe two approaches that I have found to be especially valuable in addressing different ERM objectives, company structures, and resources available to expend on ERM. Are they the only ways to do ERM? Of course not. I suspect if I continue to do ERM for another 20 years, I will find ways to continue to improve these approaches, but I also firmly believe you can use them today and achieve productive, valuable results.

While there are many activities involved in ERM, I ask that you remember some very basic yet profound truths about ERM:

Somebody, somewhere, knows something.

ERM, done right, "gets to the truth."

We, as risk specialists, must get the right information, to the right people, at the right time.

GLOSSARY

The following definitions are consistent with my real-world ERM experience and align with how I use these terms in this book. They are not necessarily the official views of The IIA or any other governing body, unless otherwise indicated.

Term	Definition
Common language	Common risk terminology used by management and employees across the organization to ensure that all personnel share the same understanding of risk.
Contributing factors	Current risk drivers, issues, root causes, and/or historical events actually driving the concern about the risk.
Enterprise risk	Any significant activity or event that could have a negative impact on achieving objectives across all categories of risk, such as strategic, operational, legal, and financial; tends to be more significant to executive management, board members, and other key stakeholders.
Enterprise risk analysis	Completed inherent risk summary form for each inherent risk in the enterprise risk inventory (for the board-confidence approach) and a completed executive summary for each enterprise risk in the inventory.
Enterprise risk assessment	Identifies the risks that matter most to the executive team and the board (risks to the execution of the enterprise's strategy and achievement of its objectives).
Enterprise risk inventory	A comprehensive list of high-level, broadly defined risk inherent to the business across all categories of risk, such as strategic, operational, legal, and financial.
Enterprise risk management (ERM)	• The culture, capabilities, and practices integrated with strategy-setting and performance that organizations rely on to manage risk in creating, preserving, and realizing value (COSO). • A provider of timely, useful risk information that helps management make decisions and effectively manage risks toward the achievement of objectives (author).

Term	Definition
Inherent risk	Any risk before considering risk management activities in place to manage the risk.
Key performance indicator (KPI)	A selected metric that provides visibility into the performance of the business and enables decision makers to take action; generally tied to a target and chosen to give an indication of performance toward achievement of goals and objectives.
Key risk indicator (KRI)	A selected metric that provides an early signal of increasing risk exposure.
Residual risk	Risk, if any, that is of concern after considering the related contributing factors and risk management activities.
Residual risk impact	The organization's residual exposure based on impact and likelihood after application of the current risk management activities.
Risk	• The possibility that events will occur and affect the achievement of strategy and business objectives (COSO). • Any potential activity or event that could have a negative impact on the achievement of objectives (author).
Risk coordinator	The highest-ranking nonexecutive in the company (often at the SVP or VP level) over an enterprise risk.
Risk owner	Highest-level executive (often an EVP) responsible for a particular enterprise risk. Sometimes used interchangeably with "risk sponsor."
Risk sponsor	Highest-level executive (often an EVP) responsible for a particular enterprise risk. Sometimes used interchangeably with "risk owner."

INTERNAL AUDIT FOUNDATION SPONSOR RECOGNITION

STRATEGIC PARTNERS

PARTNERS

PRESIDENT'S CIRCLE (US $25,000+)

Larry Harrington
CIA, QIAL, CRMA

FOUNDATION PARTNERS
(US $5,000–$14,999)

**The Estate of
Wayne G. Moore**
CIA

INTERNAL AUDIT FOUNDATION BOARD OF TRUSTEES

PRESIDENT
Michael J. Fucilli, CIA, CGAP, CRMA, QIAL, *Metropolitan Transportation Authority*

VICE PRESIDENT-STRATEGY
Scott J. Feltner, CIA, *Kohler Company*

VICE PRESIDENT—RESEARCH AND EDUCATION
Jacqueline K. Wagner, CIA, *Ernst & Young LLP*

VICE PRESIDENT—DEVELOPMENT
Carey L. Oven, CIA, *Deloitte & Touche LLP*

TREASURER
Warren W. Stippich Jr., CIA, CRMA, *Grant Thornton LLP, Chicago*

SECRETARY
Deborah F. Kretchmar, CIA, *LPL Financial*

STAFF LIAISON
Bonnie L. Ulmer, *Internal Audit Foundation*

MEMBERS

Kevin L. Cantrell, CIA, *Plains All American Pipeline*

Brian P. Christensen, *Protiviti Inc.*

Jean Coroller, *The French Institute of Directors*

Philip E. Flora, CIA, CCSA, *FloBiz & Associates, LLC*

Stephen D. Goepfert, CIA, CRMA, QIAL

Ulrich Hahn, CIA, CCSA, CGAP, CRMA

Lisa Hartkopf, *Ernst & Young LLP*

Steven E. Jameson, CIA, CCSA, CFSA, CRMA, *Community Trust Bank*

Pamela Short Jenkins, CIA, CRMA, *Fossil, Inc.*

Tow Toon Lim, CRMA, *DSO National Laboratories*

James A. Molzahn, CIA, CRMA, *Sedgwick, Inc.*

Frank M. O'Brien, CIA, QIAL, *Olin Corporation*

Sakiko Sakai, CIA, CCSA, CFSA, CRMA, *Infinity Consulting*

Tania Stegemann, CIA, CCSA, CRMA, *CIMIC Group Limited*

Anton Van Wyk, CIA, CRMA, QIAL, *PricewaterhouseCoopers LLP*

Yi Hsin Wang, CIA, CGAP, CRMA, *National Taipei University*

Ana Cristina Zambrano Preciado, CIA, CCSA, CRMA, *IIA–Colombia*

INTERNAL AUDIT FOUNDATION COMMITTEE OF RESEARCH AND EDUCATION ADVISORS

CHAIRMAN

Jacqueline K. Wagner, CIA, *Ernst & Young, LLP*

VICE CHAIRMAN

Tania Stegemann, CIA, CCSA, CRMA, *CIMIC Group Limited*

STAFF LIAISON

Larry L. Baker, CCSA, CRMA, *Internal Audit Foundation*

MEMBERS

James A. Alexander, CIA, *Unitus Community Credit Union*

Karen Begelfer, CIA, CRMA, *Sprint Corporation*

Subramanian Bhaskar, *IIA–India*

Despoina Chatzaga, CIA, CCSA, CFSA, *Exiger Limited*

Vonani Chauke, CIA, *Deloitte & Touche SA*

Angelina K. Y. Chin, CIA, CCSA, CRMA

Margaret Heim Christ, CIA, *University of Georgia*

Daniel Clayton, CIA, *University of Texas System*

Roslyn Y. Dahl, CIA, *Westfield Group*

Ozgur Baris Ekici, CIA, *Eaton Corporation*

Urban Eklund, CIA, CRMA, *Ericsson*

Carolyn Ferguson, *Texas Guaranteed Student Loan Corporation*

Stephen G. Goodson, CIA, CCSA, CGAP, CRMA, *UT Austin McCombs School*

Judy Grobler, CIA, CRMA

Kivilcim Gunbatti, *Ziraat Bank*

Yulia Gurman, CIA, *Packaging Corporation of America*

Beatrice Ki-Zerbo, CIA

Brian Daniel Lay, CRMA, *Ernst & Young LLP*

Steve Mar, CFSA

Jozua Francois Martins, CIA, CRMA, *Citizens Property Insurance Corporation*

Mani Massoomi, CFSA, CRMA, *TIAA*

Joseph A. Mauriello, CIA, CFSA, CRMA, *University of Texas at Dallas*

John D. McLaughlin, *The Audit Exchange LLC*

Mark J. Pearson, CIA

Jason Philibert, CIA, CRMA

Sundaresan Rajeswar, CIA, CCSA, CFSA, CGAP, CRMA, *Teyseer Group of Companies*

James M. Reinhard, CIA, *Simon Property Group*

Bismark Rodriguez, CIA, CCSA, CFSA, CRMA, *Financial Services Risk Management*

Hesham K. Shawa, *IIA Jordon – International*

Deanna F. Sullivan, CIA, CRMA, *SullivanSolutions*

Jason Robert Thogmartin, CIA, CRMA, *First Data Corporation*

Adriana Beatriz Toscano Rodriguez, CIA, CRMA, *UTE*

Jane Traub, CCSA, *The Nielsen Company*

Maritza Villanueva, CIA, *Regal Forest Holding*

Paul L. Walker, *St. John's University*

Larry G. Wallis, CIA, *VIA Metropolitan Transit*

Chance R. Watson, CIA, CRMA, *Texas Department of Family & Protective Services*

Klaas J. Westerling, CIA, *Intertrust Group Holding S.A.*